THE BLACK COWBOYS

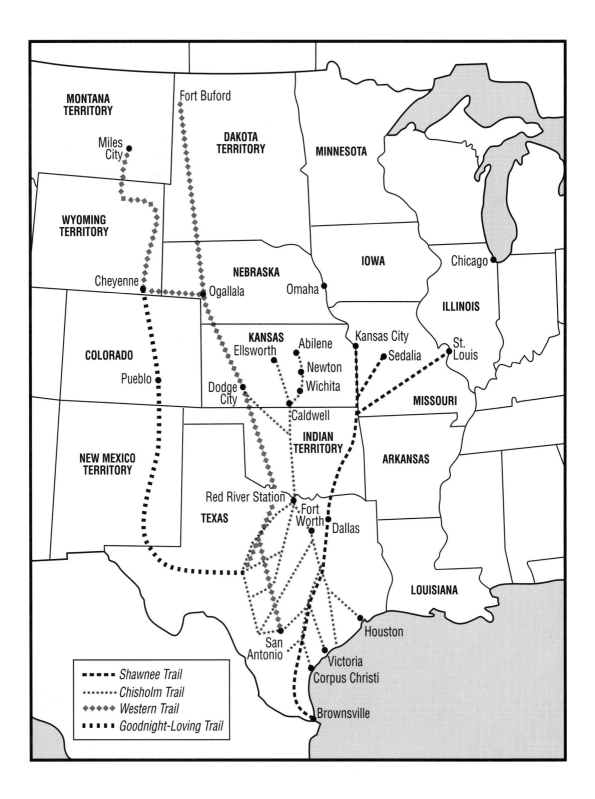

AFRICAN-AMERICAN ACHIEVERS

THE
BLACK COWBOYS

Gina De Angelis

CHELSEA HOUSE PUBLISHERS
Philadelphia

978
DEA

Chelsea House Publishers
Editor-in-Chief Stephen Reginald
Production Manager Pamela Loos
Picture Editor Judy Hasday
Art Director Sara Davis
Managing Editor Jim Gallagher
Senior Production Editor Lisa Chippendale

Staff for THE BLACK COWBOYS
Senior Editor Therese De Angelis
Associate Editor Kristine Brennan
Designer Keith Trego
Picture Researcher Patricia Burns
Cover Design Keith Trego

3 5 7 9 8 6 4

Library of Congress Cataloging-in-Publication Data T.K.

De Angelis, Gina.
   The Black cowboys / by Gina De Angelis.
   104 pp.   cm. —(African-American achievers)
   Includes bibliographical references (p. 98) and index.
   Summary: An account of the adventurous African
Americans whose exploits contributed to the legends of
the Wild West.
   ISBN 0-7910-2589-6 (hc). — ISBN 0-7910-2590-X (pb)
1. Afro-American cowboys--West (U.S.)—History—
Juvenile literature. 2. West (U.S.)—History—Juvenile
literature. 3. Frontier and pioneer life—West (U.S.)—
Juvenile literature.
[1. Afro-American cowboys. 2. West (U.S.)--History. 3.
Frontier and pioneer life—West (U.S.)] I. Title. II. Series.
F596.D36 1997
978'.00496073--dc21 97-24823
                                                    CIP
                                                    AC

*Frontis: A map tracing four of the
main trails used to move cattle from
Texas breeding grounds to railheads in
northern states.*

*On the cover: Cowboys (foreground),
Corbis-Bettmann; Cattle drive (back-
ground), Corbis-Bettmann*

21.95

CONTENTS

AFRICAN-AMERICAN ACHIEVERS

THE BLACK COWBOYS

1

Blacks in the Americas

IN 1536 A GROUP of four bedraggled and exhausted men wandered into Spanish headquarters in Mexico, their clothes torn to rags. The four men—Álvar Núñez Cabeza de Vaca, Alonso de Castillo, Andrés Dorantes, and his slave, Esteban— were the only survivors of a 500-man expedition into present-day Florida that had sailed from Spain eight years earlier. Of the long and fascinating tales they recounted, including stories of their enslavement by a coastal Indian tribe near present-day Galveston, Texas, the adventures of Esteban are perhaps most important to us: he was probably the first black explorer of America.

During his years of wandering, Esteban (sometimes called Stephen Dorantes or Estevanico) posed as a medicine man, or shaman, in order to gain safe passage and assistance from the natives he and his companions encountered. His adoption of American Indian ways earned the respect of his hosts, and he learned a great deal about traditional lore and heard tales of splendid cities. The viceroy of New Spain, Antonio de Mendoza, listened with fascination to Esteban's account of a fabulously rich region to the north called the Seven Cities of Cíbola,

A family proudly poses before their Nebraska homestead, 1887. Many African Americans headed west during the late 19th century in the hope of securing their own land and building a better, more prosperous life.

which natives had told him about. Eager to find these riches, Mendoza mounted an expedition in 1539. The famous Spanish search for Cíbola was on.

Esteban was chosen to be the guide for the expedition and was sent ahead to communicate with the natives. Once more he adopted the dress and deportment of a medicine man. He was instructed to send wooden crosses back to the main party, who would be able to tell by the increasing size of the crosses how close he was to reaching his goal. Over the next few weeks, Esteban's Indian messengers arrived with news of his growing number of followers and of gifts he had collected—and they also brought huge crosses. Fray Marcos de Niza, the expedition's leader, grew ever more excited.

But suddenly the messages from Esteban ceased. A few weeks later, Fray Marcos encountered two frightened Indian members of Esteban's retinue. From them he learned that Esteban and nearly all those with him had been killed by hostile members of the Zuni tribe.

The adventures of Esteban—one of the first non-Indians to explore the American Southwest—became part of Zuni Indian legends that are still told today. However, though many Americans know about North American explorers like Ponce de León and Hernando de Soto, very few have ever heard of black explorers like Esteban.

The 16th-century adventurer was the first of many black men to explore the North American continent. Blacks were among the first nonnatives to arrive in North America—the crews of Christopher Columbus's ships included blacks—and not all were slaves. Several accompanied Louis Joliet and Father Jacques Marquette on their fur-trapping and missionary excursion in 1673.

Another black explorer, Jean Baptiste Pointe Du Sable, was a Haitian who had been educated in Paris. Du Sable founded "Eschikagou," the first

A Hopi kachina doll (center) represents the passage of Esteban through the tribe's Arizona land. As the first black to explore the American Southwest, Esteban acquired a legendary status among the region's Native Americans that persisted long after he was gone.

permanent settlement on the site of present-day Chicago. He married a Native American woman, with whom he had two children, and turned a small fur-trading post into a profitable settlement, which he sold in 1800 for $1,200—a fortune in those days. Du Sable was arrested in 1779 by the British, who suspected that his sympathies for the French were treasonous. But the charges were ultimately dropped because of his impeccable character and the testimony of his many European and Native American friends.

Meriwether Lewis and William Clark's famous expedition into the vast Louisiana Territory included not only the famous Shoshone interpreter and guide Sacajawea, but also Clark's black slave York, who was equally valuable to the expedition.

York was the first African most Native Americans had ever seen. An imposing figure, "over six feet tall and over two hundred pounds," York befriended many Indians by allowing them to try to rub off his black color and by dancing for them and telling stories. He was a skilled hunter and fisherman, and he assisted Sacajawea as an interpreter.

In 1826 the first overland expedition to reach

California included black explorer Peter Ranne. During the mid-1800s black frontiersmen like James Beckwourth, counterparts to such legendary white explorers as Daniel Boone and Davy Crockett, helped tame the western wilderness. Freeborn in Virginia in 1798, James Beckwourth led an adventurous life in California, trapping furs, living with Crow Indians, stealing horses from wealthy ranchers, and operating a one-man pony express between Monterey and Los Angeles.

Most African Americans who went west before or during the Civil War were slaves accompanying their owners, but free blacks also headed west in the hope of building a better, more prosperous life for themselves and their children. Like their white counterparts, African-American settlers hoped to live in peace in the new territories. All too often, however, they were prevented from doing so by frightened whites who feared blacks nearly as much as they did the "savage" Indians, or those whose dream of opportunity and advancement in the West did not include "coloreds."

Arthur Barkshire, a free black resident of Indiana, was one of the many blacks to encounter such barriers in the early 19th century. Since Indiana was pursuing a non-immigration policy toward blacks, Barkshire was arrested for harboring a slave when he brought his fiancée west from Ohio. Although he appealed to the state supreme court, his marriage was deemed null and void. Another free black, Mrs. Mary Randolph, was aboard a stagecoach bound for Colorado when the driver put her off in Kansas because she was "colored." Randolph spent a terrifying night alone on the prairie with nothing but her umbrella to scare away coyotes.

A few blacks managed to prevail over such deep-seated attitudes, even in the more established East. One of the first to do so was Lucy Terry, who lived in frontier New England in the early 1700s. In

1756 she married Abijah Prince, a black man who had served for the British in the French and Indian Wars and who had been granted land in Sunderland, Vermont, by Britain's King George III. Two of their sons served in the Revolutionary War.

When Lucy and Abijah's ownership of their farm was threatened by wealthy white neighbors, she appeared before the governor's council to protest. The council found in her favor in 1785. After her husband's death, Lucy took up a second legal battle to keep the property left to her and her children; once again she was successful. Remarkably, a black woman had defeated a wealthy, politically influential white family—not once, but twice—for perhaps the first time in the history of the young country. Racist policies and attitudes

A 1908 watercolor by Charles M. Russell depicts an Indian tribe's fascination with York, Lewis and Clark's interpreter and guide. Many of the Native Americans York encountered had never seen an African before, and he good-naturedly allowed them to try to rub off his black color.

A scene from the 1950 movie Tomahawk, in which the role of black explorer James Beckwourth was played by white actor Jack Oakie (foreground).

became more institutionalized with the development of the slave industry, however, and Lucy eventually lost her farm to her white neighbors.

Although some historians claim that color barriers were erased on unsettled frontiers where survival often depended on assistance from neighbors, racism was not absent in the West. As frontier towns grew more densely settled, the attitudes and institutions of the East, including racism and slavery, spread there as well.

Despite these difficulties, blacks were welcomed in some territories. In a culture that treated them as second-class citizens at best, African Americans were often much better neighbors to Native Americans than whites were, and for this reason they were able to establish settlements in areas where the natives would not allow whites. Black missionaries John Marrant (born in 1775) and John Stewart (born in 1790), for example, traveled west to convert Native Americans to Christianity in the late 18th and early 19th centuries. They were so successful among western tribes that their home churches subsequently sent other blacks to continue their work.

African Americans participated in the European migration westward as mountain men, scouts, fur traders, miners, farmers, missionaries, soldiers, cowboys, outlaw gunslingers, law officers, "con" men, ranchers, schoolteachers, businessmen, and politicians, among other occupations. They encountered the same hardships on the frontier as did European Americans and often endured the additional pain of racism and persecution. Although some prospered, many more did not. And though many of them left no historical traces, they all helped transform what is now the western United States.

The achievements of Esteban, York, Du Sable, Beckwourth, and others help tell the story of the African-American experience in America. These men and countless other men and women, though often absent from the pages of history books, were instrumental in the founding of America.

In 1950 Universal Pictures released a western entitled *Tomahawk*, which told the story of the discovery of a pass through the Sierra Nevada mountains that had been discovered by James Beckwourth. But although the role was played by a white actor, the real James Beckwourth, an army scout, hunter, trapper, gold prospector, and fighter, was black.

Beckwourth spent his life on the frontier of America and lived among many Native American tribes; he was even a Crow chief for several years. He was one of the guides forced to help the U.S. Army find its way to the Cheyenne and Arapaho

A group of Exodusters wait on a riverbank for a steamboat to carry them westward. Between 1878 and 1881, thousands of black southerners heeded the call of "Pap" Singleton and Henry Adams to migrate to Kansas.

settlement near Sand Creek in southeastern Colorado, where in 1864 at least 130 men, women, and children were killed in a surprise attack by the Colorado militia.

In 1854, Beckwourth dictated to T. D. Bonner his autobiography, *The Life and Adventures of James P. Beckwourth, Mountaineer, Scout, Pioneer, and Chief of the Crow Nation*, which was published two years later. Though his exploits and skills earned him renown, many of his stories were "tall tales"—stories purportedly true but so outrageous as to be physically impossible. Thus his own accounts were always considered somewhat untrustworthy. Nevertheless, tall tales are an integral part of frontier history and culture, and Beckwourth, like Daniel Boone and Davy Crockett, is an American legend. Although his story, like theirs, is peppered with such tales, it contains a core of truth.

The stories of another black mountain man named Edward Rose—a contemporary of Beckwourth—were also considered unreliable, though his character was not. In his 1848 book *The Five Scalps*, Captain Ruben Holmes of the U.S. Army described him this way:

> Rose possessed qualities, both physical and mental, that soon gained him the respect of the Indians. He loved fighting for its own sake. He seemed in strife almost recklessly and desperately to seek death where it was most likely to be found. No Indian ever preceded him in the attack or pursuit of an enemy . . . He was as cunning as the prairie wolf. He was a perfect woodsman. He could endure any kind of fatigue and privation as well as the best trained Indians. He studied men. There was nothing that an Indian could do, that Rose did not make himself master of. He knew all that Indians knew. He was a great man in his situation.

Rose was much in demand as a scout and interpreter. Beckwourth credited him with saving their 1825 expedition from Indian attack by befriending the Indians. He was also expert at hunting and trapping, essential skills for survival in the unsettled West.

The fur traders of the early 19th century were more than just "mountain men" or rough-hewn entrepreneurs; they were also instrumental in the exploration of the American West. In many cases, they were the first non-Indian men to explore certain areas. They often developed good relations with local Indians; at times they joined their settlements and took Native American wives. Their knowledge of the customs and languages of various tribes made them invaluable interpreters and negotiators. And their detailed knowledge of the land, which they imparted to mapmakers, provided essential information for the settlers who eventually followed.

But fur traders and mountain men usually did not want to see the West settled; in fact, when the area in which they worked became too "civilized" or populous, they would often move farther west to pursue the wilderness life they loved.

The first major wave of black emigration from the South—the "Exodus," as its participants called it—consisted of about 50,000 people who settled in Kansas between 1878 and 1881. These travelers named their migration after the Bible's second book, an account that many blacks treasured because it depicts the Israelites escaping from a bondage African Americans saw as similar to their own.

Some of the Exodusters, as they became known, journeyed to Kansas on their own initiative. But the majority went at the urging of two men, Benjamin "Pap" Singleton of Tennessee and Henry Adams of Louisiana. Earnest advocates of emigration, both men proposed the same solution to the problems faced by southern blacks, and both used similar means—handbills, meetings, speeches —to spark interest in the Exodus. But in other ways they differed. They never met and never even sought to coordinate their efforts by mail. Instead, each recruited largely from his home state (although some Exodusters came from Texas, Mississippi, and Alabama).

Singleton had spent most of his life as a slave and had managed to escape the South before emancipation. From that point on he resolved to help blacks become what he called "safe and secure." He moved back to Tennessee and became a carpenter. When the backlash against blacks began during the 1870s, he concluded that he had a God-given mission to lead his race out of the former slave states.

Because Reconstruction gains were so limited for Tennessee's black residents, Singleton began making arrangements for them to travel to Kansas. By 1876 he had set up a company, called the Edgefield Real Estate Association, and after two years of proposing migration at festivals, picnics, and religious gatherings, he began leading groups of blacks west.

Henry Adams took a different route. A younger man than Singleton, he had spent his formative years during Reconstruction, watching blacks acquire considerable power in Louisiana through the political process. He became a local political leader himself, serving a constituency of poor black farmers. Adams did not claim divine inspiration for his mission; instead, he believed he was fulfilling his duty to represent his working-class followers. At first he counseled blacks to move to Liberia—a West African colony established in 1821 by wealthy white abolitionists for freed American slaves. But in 1879, after conditions had become especially bad in the South and after some blacks had already resettled in Kansas, he became a prime advocate of the Exodus.

Singleton and Adams both urged Exodusters to establish farming towns separate from those of whites in order to strengthen their self-sufficiency and racial pride. In early 1878 the migration was still a slow stream. But in the wake of the vicious election of 1878, in which black voters were discouraged from voting by threats, shootings, and other violence, the stream became a torrent. Thousands of black families found themselves caught up in what was called "Kansas Fever." Eventually, Exodusters established several new all-black towns in Kansas, the largest of which, Nicodemus, boasted more than 700 residents.

To get to Kansas, Exodusters had to overcome fierce resistance from white southern authorities. Employers—even though they insisted that blacks were inferior beings unworthy of full citizenship—valued them as an essential source of manual work, and they feared that a labor shortage would develop if too many blacks left the area. One of the ways in which they attempted to prevent the migration was to persuade law enforcement officials to arrest traveling blacks and charge them with vagrancy. Some states passed laws making it illegal for "outside agitators" such as Singleton to lure blacks from their jobs. Others hired thugs to intimidate and beat recruiters for the Exodus, and they strong-armed steamboat companies into refusing black passengers.

Those who did make it out of the South also encountered racial abuse, but it was of a different order from that of the regions they had left behind. There were far fewer violent incidents and far less interference with black political rights in Kansas and Oklahoma, the Exodusters' main destinations.

In smaller numbers, black emigrants also headed for the far West. There, as some African Americans had been doing for several decades, they participated in such fabled aspects of western settlement as gold rushes, cattle drives, Indian fights, and fur trapping. The common image of the Old West as primarily white is inaccurate. It was actually a place of great ethnic variety, featuring a mixture of Native Americans, Chinese Americans, Mexican Americans, African Americans, and whites.

A number of the earliest black settlers in the West attained distinction, prominence, and financial success. George Washington, for example, the founder of the town of Centralia, Washington, was the son of a white mother and a slave father. Born in 1817, he was formally adopted by a white family, who moved from his native Virginia to Ohio and then to Missouri, where he was granted almost all the rights of a citizen. Washington then traveled with his foster family to Oregon Territory in 1850, where his adoptive father purchased a 640-acre parcel of land for him. Because of the territory's antiblack laws, however, Washington was not allowed to hold the rights to the land. White settlers in the area circulated petitions on Washington's behalf, and in 1852 the Oregon legislature passed a special law that enabled him to stay in the territory and keep the land. He became a successful farmer and married a black woman named Mary Jane Cooness in 1867 (he remarried in 1890, two years after her death, and had a son shortly after).

George Washington not only founded the town of Centralia, Washington; he also saved the town from ruin during the financial panic of 1893 by importing food from as far away as Portland, Oregon, and by providing jobs for unemployed townspeople.

When the Northern Pacific Railroad charted a course through his land in 1872, Washington decided to found a town called Centerville, midway between the Columbia River and Puget Sound. He donated land for churches, schools, and a cemetery as well as for individual settlers. During the financial panic of 1893, Washington saved the town, becoming "a one-man relief agency" that provided food and jobs for impoverished residents. When Washington died in an accident in 1905, the mayor of the town, now called Centralia, declared a day of mourning. He was buried in the cemetery that he had donated.

Another African American, George Bonga, was

As a slave in the South, "Aunt" Clara Brown saw her husband and their three children sold to different slave-owners. After purchasing her own freedom, she headed west, trying for years to earn enough money to free her family. She became one of the leading citizens of Central City, Colorado, where she is still honored today.

a prominent citizen of Minnesota who, like his father and grandfather, was a successful fur trader. His grandparents were slaves who had come to Minnesota with their British owner, an army officer, in the late 1700s, and his father, also a slave, was a trusted worker who was often left in charge of his owner's trading post while his owner was away. The son of a Chippewa woman, George, who was born a freeman in 1802, also married a Chippewa. Like his father, he sometimes served as an Indian interpreter when necessary, and according to William Loren Katz, author of *The Black West*, he knew "English, French, Chippewa and several other Indian languages." George was hired by the governor of Minnesota as an interpreter for local Indian tribes while continuing to work in the fur trading business.

"Aunt" Clara Brown was taken west as a slave when she was three years old. After purchasing her own freedom, she continued traveling west, trying to earn enough money to free her family. When she was 59 she traveled with a caravan of settlers heading for Denver, Colorado. After helping to found a Sunday school there, Brown moved to Central City, Colorado, where she opened a laundry. She eventually amassed 10 thousand dollars and had investments in mining claims. Although she was never able to locate her immediate family after the Civil War, she did sponsor several wagon trains to take other African Americans—many of whom were her relatives—to the West.

John Jones, born in North Carolina to a white father and a free black mother, traveled with his wife to the bustling frontier city of Chicago in 1845, where he became an uncommonly successful businessman. His fortune and his good reputation among neighbors and acquaintances helped him to use his home as a way station for the Underground Railroad, and he fought the "black laws" of Illinois that barred black immigration into the state. He was twice elected to the Cook County Board of Commissioners. Wealthy and highly respected, Jones risked a great deal by speaking out, and many less fortunate blacks were persuaded by his example to lend themselves to the cause.

The city of Los Angeles was founded in part by free blacks. Maria Rita Valdez, the granddaughter of two black residents, owned Rancho Rodeo de las Aguas, today's Beverly Hills. Pio Pico, a man of black and Hispanic blood, served as governor of California in the 1840s. Others, such as William Robinson, who was a rider for the famous and now legendary Pony Express, and George Monroe, a well-known stagecoach driver and the son of a California prospector, were among the African Americans who successfully overcame racism and prejudice. Another, Mifflin Gibbs, who shined shoes in Colorado during its wild days, became the first black judge in the United States. And Mrs. Biddy Mason, who had walked behind her master's wagons from Missouri to California, successfully sued for her and her daughters' freedom and generously donated time, money, and land to establish African-American schools and churches in California.

These little-known histories are among many that illustrate the important role of African Americans in the westward expansion of America. But some of the most famous—and exciting—tales of the founding of the West concern the accomplishments of the American cowboy. And among these accounts are the outrageous and brave exploits of black cowboys.

2

The Birth of the American Cowboy

COWBOYS DID NOT LEAD the lives portrayed in most movies about the Old West. They were not the only "real Americans" in the country. They did not spend their time chasing down villains, having shootouts with Indians and Mexicans, and rescuing women from danger. Real cowboys worked strenuously at jobs that were so physically taxing that some died while working. They spent little time in established towns; most often, they were on the range for months, sleeping on the ground and spending days on horseback, with little company other than their fellow cowhands. While working on ranches, they would spend weeks at a time alone or with one or two others. Cowgirls were virtually nonexistent, although on small ranches women would help with riding and handling livestock during busy seasons.

Southeasterners had been raising cattle since colonial times, but the cattle industry's real heyday began after the Civil War. It was at this point that entrepreneurs discovered that they could make a for-

A cowboy oversees the herd during a cattle drive in the late 19th century.

Trail drivers take a day off in the cattle town of Cheyenne, Wyoming.

tune by transporting cattle from the West—where almost unlimited grazing land made the raising of huge herds not only possible but economical—to the East, where demand for beef created soaring prices and immense profits. Because railroad lines were just starting to make their way into the West, cattle had to be driven hundreds of miles overland to such railway connections as Abilene and Dodge City, Kansas, from which the cattle were transported to eastern markets.

This driving was the job of the cowboys, who also tended the cattle on the grasslands of the Plains. It was not an easy venture, but few industries required as little manpower. Those who took on the work had to be competent, trustworthy, and loyal—and willing to brave great danger. Thousands of dollars of the cattle owner's money rested in their hands.

In frontier regions where populations were scant, entrepreneurs usually encountered a shortage of labor. For this reason, cowboys were relatively well paid; most earned $20 to $30 monthly. Trail bosses and foremen were paid $50 to $60 each month. Cooks, whose duties were among the most essential but whose status was just above that of horse wrangler, received about $50.

After the Civil War, when the cattle industry expanded, an exceptionally skilled cowboy might demand $35 to $45 a month. In addition to regular wages, cowboys received board (or food) and were supplied with four to six horses each. They might receive bonuses for bringing their own mounts to the job, but they were expected to supply their own saddles, bridles, and other riding equipment.

During the 1870s and 1880s, while the range cattle industry was expanding, skilled and even novice cowboys were in great demand. After the 1890s, however, as fences were erected and fewer hands were required, work became more scarce. Less talented—and less honest—cowboys might have "rustled" or stolen cattle to make their living.

Still, an experienced cowhand could nearly always find work. Out of season, he might live cost-free with a cattle outfit or on a ranch, provided he agreed to work for the outfit the following spring. This practice was known as "riding the grub-line." Those who were extremely thrifty might save up enough to start their own ranches or farms, but none became wealthy.

On the other hand, very few of them had wives or children to support, and necessities like boots, chaps, spurs, saddles, pistols, bandannas, hats, and horses could be acquired as cheaply or as expensively as each cowboy's tastes dictated. Although some would spend several months' pay during a night in town, others might simply have a few drinks and ride back to camp.

John Clay, a man who worked on cattle ranches for many years, saw some cattlemen save their money and later settle down to become responsible citizens. But he never saw an old cowpuncher; "where they disappeared to remained a mystery." The physical strain of the work took an especially heavy toll on older men, even more so on those who had suffered injuries in earlier years.

Among the roughly 30,000 cowboys of the Old West were more than 5,000 black cowboys who worked in the open-range industry between 1866 and 1896. The majority came west during the 1870s, impelled by racial oppression and by the shortage of economic opportunities for blacks in the Southeast.

Even as cowboys, blacks could not completely escape discrimination, however. They rarely had, for example, the same chance as their white peers to advance from common cowhand to foreman or trail boss. They made up a high proportion of workers in the two jobs with the least status—cook and horse wrangler. And, when they sought respite in town from the rigors of the trail, they did not enjoy the same freedom as whites: in saloons they were relegated to one end of the bar and were usually forbidden the company of white prostitutes. In addition, they were sometimes subjected to pranks and name-calling; a black crew member might end up being called "Nigger Newt" or "Nigger Bob."

In some towns, however, profit may have been the only common denominator. The famous African-American cowboy Nat Love remarked that, despite segregated bars, he was in other ways always treated in the same way as whites and that all were welcome in the saloons "for as long as our money held out."

Overall, black cowboys probably encountered less abuse than blacks in other occupations. They received the same pay as white cowboys, slept in the same bunkhouses, and ate the same food. Cowboys worked in close proximity, gathering together around the fire at night and performing cooperative tasks during the day. This closeness disposed white cowboys to see their black peers as individual human beings rather than as abstract stereotypes. In cattle driving and ranch work, skill counted more than skin color.

The great distance between the cattle trails and civilization also cut white cowboys off from the racist ideologies gaining force in the East. The exceptional courage and strength with which black cowboys performed their tasks greatly impressed their white comrades. And because each cowboy had to depend on the rest of his crew, white cowboys were discouraged from mistreating blacks.

If the work was hard and lonely and the wages were merely competitive, why would anyone want to be a cowboy? To satisfy one's spirit of adventure, for one thing. On the trail drives, cowboys encountered hostile Indians, rattlesnakes, and other dangers. They tackled the hazards of working with horses and cattle—fording rivers, preventing or halting stampedes—all while enjoying or enduring the elements under an enormous open sky. This "rugged and picturesque life," as one historian describes it, also provided the opportunity to travel throughout the country and experience what most people would never have the chance to see: the Great Plains, the Rocky Mountains, mighty rivers, thundering herds of buffalo, and exotic Native Americans. A cowboy could see manmade wonders as well: railroads under construction and cattle towns and mining cities that seemed to spring up overnight. And though the work may have been punishing, the life of a cowboy was flexible: he never had to settle down, and he could change jobs with every season if he wished (although most showed great loyalty to one outfit or rancher).

It was difficult for an inexperienced cowboy to "earn his spurs" and become a respected member of a crew. In addition to the complicated tasks he had to master, all new men were subjected to a sort of "hazing" process. No one knows whether African-American cowboys were hazed more often or more harshly than whites, but generally any new man who took the joking well and laughed along with the others would be accepted in time.

Most historians agree that there was little fighting among black and white cowboys. On the contrary, stories abound of white cowboys defending their black colleagues from discrimination—and sometimes narrowly avoiding arrest—in the cattle towns and on the trail or the ranch. In their book *The Negro Cowboys*, Philip Durham and Everett Jones recount one tale:

> One [African-American cowhand] walked down a Dodge [City] street with Bill Sparks, a white cowboy who had ridden with him up the trail from Texas. They were stopped by a drunk, "who began to abuse the Negro for no apparent reason other than he appeared to be colored." Not wanting trouble, the Negro did nothing, but Sparks took up the quarrel and fought and won a fight with the drunk. No sooner was that fight finished than Sparks was accosted by a middle-aged cattleman who berated him for siding with "a nigger." When Sparks defended himself and his friend the second time, the cattleman knocked Sparks out with a loaded quirt [a riding whip]. After he came to, Sparks got a coupling pin and cold-cocked the cowman. Later the two men, having discussed the issue in forthright Dodge City fashion, became friends.

Like most people who lived on the frontier, cowboys lived by a code of honesty and hospitality that many easterners found remarkable. It was not unusual for stray cattle found on the trail to be sold at trail's end and the proceeds sent to their rightful owner—who would have been identified, of course,

by the brand on the cattle. Similarly, a traveler could stop at any ranch house to ask for food and lodging—even for several days—and expect it to be given cheerfully and without charge. Passersby were expected to help themselves in the kitchen or pantry if no one was home, provided they clean up after themselves. In a dangerous and sparsely settled country where hotels and restaurants were hundreds of miles apart, such unwritten laws were more than matters of simple etiquette—a traveler's very life might depend upon them.

Black cowboys seemed to have a special gift for handling and riding horses, which was perhaps a legacy of slavery, under which they had primary

One of the advantages of life on the trail was the opportunity to view natural marvels such as this canyon in Crow territory in Montana.

19th-century artist Frederick Remington's sketch of black jockeys.

responsibility for the stables on plantations. Among the first black cowboys were also slaves who had learned their skills in Texas from Mexican cowboys, called *vaqueros*, and those who had worked for Native American slave owners in Indian Territory in present-day Oklahoma.

Before the Civil War, in fact, many slaveowners concerned about their "property" often tried to protect their slaves from the more dangerous duties of a cowhand, such as breaking in wild horses. Durham and Jones relate one such incident:

> White bronc-busters frequently were hired to ride bucking outlaw horses; they sat in dangerous saddles, taking the shocks of bucking, sometimes bleeding from nose and mouth, sometimes fainting, risking rupture, mutilation or death. . . . One day in 1853, when [Bradford] Grimes and [Abel "Shanghai"] Pierce were working with an all-Negro crew of

cowhands, they started to break a particularly unruly stallion. A Negro roped him, and Abel Pierce held the horse's head while the horse was saddled and a Negro cowboy mounted. When the horse was released, it went off in high jumps, spinning and jolting its rider. Just then, according to one account, "a high-pitched voice called from the ranch house: 'Bradford! Bradford! Put Abel on the bad 'uns. Those Negroes are worth a thousand dollars apiece. One might get killed!' "

Having learned such skills as slaves, many blacks who traveled west to work on the Plains were already adept at breaking and riding horses and roping and branding cattle. In some cases, they also knew the duties of a ranch supervisor. Black cowboys also played an important role when horse racing became popular in the West during the late 1800s. In Idaho, for example, one of the leading horse racers during the 1870s was a former cowboy named Silver Walker. The winning jockey of the first Kentucky Derby, held in 1875, was also black.

Perhaps the greatest jockey of the 19th century was "Ike" Murphy, who began racing horses in 1875 while still a teenager. Seven years later, he won 49 of 51 races at Saratoga, New York. Before his death at age 35, he had won the Kentucky Derby three times: in 1884, 1890, and 1891.

Jimmie Winkfield, another renowned black jockey, was the last African-American to win the Kentucky Derby, in 1902 (he had also won the derby the previous year). By the early 1900s, as horse racing became a more lucrative and therefore more closely regulated sport, discrimination began to overshadow talent, and fewer white horse owners and race sponsors were willing to allow black jockeys on the track.

Not all blacks living in Texas were former slaves. Among the handful of free blacks who earned their living raising cattle in eastern Texas was Aaron

A black cowboy prepares to brand a calf while his colleagues hold the animal down. Ranch and trail duties demanded that cowboys live and work closely with one another; for this reason, black cowboys usually encountered less discrimination than blacks in other occupations.

Ashworth, who had arrived in the region in 1833, before Texas was admitted to the Union and before it became a republic. Eventually he owned more than 2,500 head of cattle, as well as several slaves. He had become so successful and had made so many influential friends that by the time Texas required all free blacks to leave the state, he was able to receive an exemption.

The earliest cattle drives took place in the 1840s, when Texans drove herds of longhorns east into Louisiana. During the California gold rush of 1849, a small beef market also developed near San Francisco. The few drives to California were extremely hazardous—and very profitable.

The greatest market for beef at the time lay to the north and east. One cattleman, Edward Piper, drove a herd north into Ohio in 1846, during the Spanish-American War. On the whole, however, such drives were considered far too hazardous to be profitable, and Texas cattlemen viewed the expansion of their herds as a liability rather than as a means for profit in this limited market.

During the four years of the Civil War, scores of calves in these Texas herds grew to be "wild cows and longhorned bulls—unbranded, unclaimed, untamed and dangerous," relate Durham and Jones. Following Reconstruction, many cattlemen returned home from the war to discover their millions of heads of unmarked cattle scattered across the plains. For skilled cowhands, work was plentiful—and even tougher than usual. One might spend weeks alone tracking down steers that had hidden themselves in the brush. One black cowboy, Henry Beckwith, developed tracking skills so refined that he was dubbed the Coyote. Traveling with only coffee, chili juice, and dried beef and cornmeal for provisions, he slept very little and carried no bedroll or blanket. His only tools were ropes to capture steers.

As Americans returned to their farms and businesses after the war and as southerners in particular began to rebuild, Texas herds swelled with wild cattle that were being reclaimed and branded. In the far North and in the East, the market for beef began to flourish. Closer to Texas, railroads were just beginning to extend into the West, finally providing a workable way to ship cattle. With millions of head of cattle and very little other property, Texas cattlemen devoted themselves to driving their herds to meet the markets in these regions. These early routes were long and arduous and demanded bone-aching and dangerous work from cowboys. But the profits for those who succeeded were well worth the trouble. So the cowboys drove the herds north and east, blazing trails for others to follow.

3

Cowboy's Work

AS THE EASTERN and northern beef markets expanded and cattle owners drove their herds to railroad terminals, a system of trails developed across the Plains. The earliest ones—like the Shawnee Trail, which passed through that tribe's land—were extremely rough, very hazardous, and at times downright impassable. In addition to avoiding natural obstacles, cowboys had to herd cattle through heavily populated areas of Indian Territory, avoiding hostile Native American tribes. Equally as dangerous were bands of armed men who feared that the fever sometimes carried by Texas cattle would spread to their own cattle or that their crops would be trampled by passing herds. These settlers often used force to prevent cattle drives from passing through.

The Chisholm Trail, named after an early trader and guide, was the first to be widely used. It was blazed in 1867 and maintained by the efforts of a young cattle dealer named Joseph G. McCoy, who had established a market and shipping center on the western edge of the Kansas settlements. The Kansas

A cattle roundup on a ranch in Union Park, Colorado.

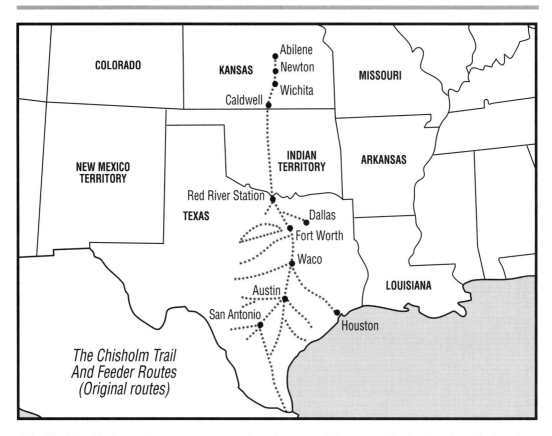

COLORADO

KANSAS

MISSOURI

Abilene
Newton
Wichita
Caldwell

NEW MEXICO
TERRITORY

INDIAN
TERRITORY

ARKANSAS

Red River Station

TEXAS

Dallas
Fort Worth

Waco

LOUISIANA

Austin

San Antonio

Houston

*The Chisholm Trail
And Feeder Routes
(Original routes)*

The Chisholm Trail was the first cattle trail to be widely used. As it grew more popular, numerous "feeder routes" sprouted from the main path.

state law barring Texas cattle had a loophole that allowed the cattle to enter the western half of the state. Aware of the loophole, McCoy persuaded the Union Pacific Railroad to build a 100-car switch near a small town called Abilene. There he constructed a stockyard that held more than 1,000 head of cattle, with pens and feed lots that held several thousand more. By setting up this shipping point, McCoy established a fixed marketplace where buyers and cattlemen could meet to conduct business. He erected a hotel for the cattlemen to stay in and a livery stable to house their horses.

McCoy then publicized the town widely, sending representatives to the Indian Nations and Texas to spread the word about the new marketplace. Thus Abilene became the terminus of the highly profitable Chisholm Trail.

The main stem of the Chisholm Trail ran from the Rio Grande River through Austin, Waco, and Fort Worth, Texas. Smaller "feeder" trails leading off of the main route went into east and west Texas. North of Fort Worth the trail lay far west of the Shawnee Trail and went through less heavily settled portions of Indian Territory and into mostly unsettled portions of Kansas. Although trail drivers following the Chisholm were still vulnerable to raids by native Comanche, they were mostly safe from extortion by black or Native American settlements and from the animosity of the Kansas homesteaders they occasionally encountered on the Shawnee trail. The trail was well-watered and good for grazing, and except during flood season the rivers were easily forded. The Chisholm Trail quickly became the preferred route for cattle drivers.

But though a good trail like the Chisholm was routinely followed—most cattle drivers logged 10 to 15 miles a day on it—there were also good reasons for turning off a trail. When grazing land or water became scarce, an entire drive would be forced to detour, often several miles off the trail. After repeated use, these alternate stretches became clearly visible, and a trail boss encountering such forks had to be highly competent to determine which path was the original and whether or not to take the detour.

Each cattle drive included about eight cowhands, a cook, a trail boss, and a wrangler. In the early days of trail driving, the owner might also serve as trail boss. On later drives, the owner usually assigned a trustworthy right-hand man to accompany the cattle to market.

The average herd included up to 2,500 head of cattle. Though some records mention much larger drives—one of more than 15,000 head, 200 people, and 1,200 horses reportedly traveled from southern Texas to California in 1869—such oversized drives were comparatively few and must have been

Texas cattle are penned and loaded onto railroad cars to be shipped east. Between 1865 and 1885, an estimated 9 to 10 million head of cattle were moved along Texas trails to livestock markets in the East, North, and West.

extremely unwieldy. On the other hand, a herd of less than 2,500 head would be too costly to drive, since the number of cowboys and horses had to be limited and the owner would incur the same labor expenses regardless of the herd's size.

According to an estimate by Edward Dale in his book *Cow Country*, more than five million head of cattle were driven north and east from Texas between 1866 and 1885, and the drives continued with less frequency for another ten years or so after that.

Cattle drives consisted of one of several different kinds of herds. The most common was a beef herd, made up of steers to be sold for meat. Under ideal conditions, a beef herd could travel 10 to 15 miles a day. The pace of a drive was important: to travel too quickly would be to risk having the cattle lose weight; moving too slowly might prevent the drive from reaching its destination before the weather turned colder. Each drive lasted about two or three months—longer if stampedes, flooded rivers, Indian attacks, cowboy deaths, or other mishaps impeded it, or if the destination was Montana, the Dakotas, California, or other far-flung regions.

Another type of herd, called a "wet herd," consisted only of milk cows. Drives of wet herds set off very early in the spring and could not travel as far or as fast as a beef herd. On such drives, cows gave birth to calves nearly every day. Trail bosses of wet herds sometimes assigned a cowhand to drive a wagon that carried the newborn animals during the day. When the herd bedded down at night, these calves would be returned to their mothers. This worker was also responsible for cutting out the calves in the morning, so he had to be a good roper as well.

A third type, a mixed herd, was the most difficult and dangerous to control because it included full-grown steers and calves, who traveled more slowly than adult animals. For this reason, drivers often found it next to impossible to save the calves. Before the drive started, a crew member was assigned to cut out the calves that were too young to travel. These calves would then be given away. The cowhand was responsible not only for cutting out calves but for shooting them when they could not be given away. At night, he had to "hobble" the mothers to prevent them from turning back to retrieve their lost calves. By tying one or more of the animal's hooves to a stake driven into the ground, the cowhand allowed her to move about to graze, but not to wander off.

One cowhand assigned to such work was a black man named Frank. Frank was only one of many black men employed by a man named Ab Blocker, but he turned out to be his most valuable employee when he saved Blocker's life during a mixed-herd drive. Durham and Jones tell how Frank rescued his boss during a lunch break on the trail:

> Frank rode into camp, threw the bridle reins over his horse's head and climbed off to get a cup of coffee. Just then Ab Blocker, who had walked away from the camp, yelled for help. Frank looked up and saw Ab running with a steer after him. Frank "threw down his cup, ran to his horse, tossed the bridle over his head and jumped in the saddle. It was the quickest, prettiest thing I nearly ever saw," [reported an onlooker]. . . . "The steer had tucked its head to hook Ab when Frank rode up behind it, whirled the rope around his head one time, and hollered, 'Hold on, boss, don't go no fu'ther.' He threw the rope over the steer's horns, the horse sat down and the steer changed ends. His tail was almost touching Ab."

Whether the drive was a beef herd, a wet herd, or a mixed herd, assembling it, the crew, the remuda (or herd of horses), and the supplies and chuck wagon for a drive entailed several weeks of preparation. Cutting out the cattle to go on the drive took days or weeks, and the work was far from over once the herd was assembled:

> Every large ranchman usually owned cattle of at least two or three brands. This made it necessary that the animals be "road branded" before starting . . . by running them through a chute and branding them lightly with a bar or slash on the shoulder, side or hip.

The skills and duties of ranch work were very different from those required on a cattle drive, though they could be equally backbreaking. Besides branding calves, the most important duties of the range rider included riding the line, driving trail herds, participating in the roundup, and selecting animals to be sold for beef. In addition, cowboys had to break or tame wild horses, hunt wolves, defend the ranch against cattle thieves, and build corrals for the herds.

Additionally, a cowhand also took care of per-

sonal chores while living out on the line, such as gathering firewood, cooking, collecting and storing clean water, washing laundry, and caring for his horse and riding gear. To make time to complete all of his own chores, the cowboy became remarkably resourceful and extremely independent. Although a cowboy depended on his fellow cowhands while working, ultimately he could rely only on himself to ensure his survival.

Like cowboys themselves, the horses they rode had to be skilled in performing specific tasks. For example, a good "cutting horse" would be able to separate a particular animal from the herd with little or no assistance from its rider. A roping horse would assist the cowboy in throwing his lariat around a steer's head or feet by stopping short at the exact moment that the rider threw the rope. Such horses were great boons to cowboys at roundup

A herd of about 3,000 head travels through Arizona, led by two cowboys at point (far left and lower right). Four swing and flank cowboys can be seen in the middle distance.

time, which occurred each spring and fall and at other times when the cattle had to be gathered in one place for buying and selling.

Between roundups or when he was not on a cattle drive, a cowboy had other work to do. Most often this consisted of "riding the line"—checking boundaries between his employer's and another's land to keep cows within grazing lands defined by the common law of the range. This unspoken rule was known as "cow custom." Even after the early 1880s, when owners began erecting wire fences to separate properties, line riding was still necessary, though perhaps a bit easier to manage.

Line riding was a lonely and monotonous job.

The cowboy had to attend to the invisible line dividing one cattle owner's land from another by repairing any fences and keeping the cattle on the correct side of the line. He was also responsible for rescuing cows from water holes and mud, protecting the herd from wolves, thieves, "screw worms," and other parasites and injuries, maintaining his camp, and extending hospitality without question to anyone who ventured into the territory.

While cowhands worked on cutting and branding the herd, the cattle owner selected the driving crew. On small ranches, most or all of the hired hands would accompany the herd. In larger outfits, some of which employed up to 200 cowboys, the hands were selected according to level of skill. First, the owner chose a trail boss, who had to be loyal beyond question and skilled enough to have won the respect of the other men. A trail boss was responsible not only for the cattle but also for the lives of his men. He had to be capable of finding established trails and judging when to turn off of them. A model trail boss was quick-witted, strong-limbed, honest, and resourceful beyond the levels expected of the other men on the crew—and he might earn up to $125 a month, comparable to ranch foreman wages.

After the trail boss or foreman, the cook was the most important man on a drive, and he was more highly paid than the riders on the drive because of his unique responsibilities. Dale describes the life of a trail cook:

> He must get up an hour before daylight each morning in order to have breakfast ready by dawn, must wash and store away the dishes three times a day, prepare food that was satisfying [under the most trying weather conditions], and must in addition be able to drive and handle four temperamental mules. . . . A good camp cook was a treasure worthy of admiration and respect, which he usually received in full store.

While the trail herd was being cut and branded and crew members selected, the owner gathered supplies to last up to four months and a vehicle, called a chuck wagon, to transport them. A large box held most of the groceries on its shelves and rested on the back of the wagon. The back wall of the box folded down to make a preparation table—an ingenious arrangement that saved space and made the cook's job easier. A ten-gallon water keg was also attached to the wagon bed, while a sling made of blankets or cowhide, holding firewood and wood chips, hung underneath it. Inside the wagon the cook stored the remaining food, along with the crew's bedrolls and personal possessions, a small toolbox, and a basic first-aid kit. Racks along the inside of the wagon held cooking pots, pans, and utensils.

Provisions for a cattle drive usually included coffee beans, molasses, beans, bacon, flour, salt, baking powder or soda, dried fruit, rice, and sugar; sometimes pickles, onions, canned tomatoes, and corn were also stocked. A good cook was usually a good fisherman and hunter as well, and he would vary the menu by relying on the natural resources of the region in which the crew camped.

Generally, cooks were viewed as an ornery breed. They had to maintain camp, collect and prepare food, and serve regular meals, regardless of weather, outside danger, or other circumstances that might hinder the rest of the trail crew in their work. The pressure of these duties earned them a reputation for crankiness. They were also accorded an exceptional measure of respect, regardless of their race. A cowboy named Jack Thorp described the hazards of aggravating a trail cook:

> [A]nyone riding up to the [chuck] wagon was supposed to approach behind the fire so that no sand would blow into the skillets and ovens. Any green puncher who, not knowing this law, violated it, was likely to learn it soon enough, by being told the

names of his ancestors and kinfolk. . . . Failure to treat [the cook] with consideration could be punished in too many ways: an erring cowboy found his coffee weak, his beans cold and hard, his meat full of gristle, his bedroll misplaced, his comfort disturbed by count-less accidents.

A trail outfit camped on the Plains near a water hole, circa 1890.

The job of a cook was lonely and hazardous as well. Since the chuck wagon rode ahead of the herd, the cook would be the first to face hostile natives or other dangers, and he nearly always had to carry a gun. As a result, many cooks became exceptional marksmen.

The lowest in rank of the cattle-driving crew was the horse wrangler, often a boy of 14 or older, whose job was to look after the horses. Each trail rider was supplied with 5 to 10 horses, a total of 45 to 90 head per drive. The wrangler rounded up these horses each morning and drove them into a makeshift corral where each rider would catch his mount for the day. Wranglers also rounded up horses at noon and at the end of each workday so that every rider had access to at least one horse for night duty or emergencies.

Although all cowboys had to ride and rope well, some men were known to have less common—and often more useful—talents. One might, for example, have unusually good vision or an excellent memory that would enable him to identify the brands on strange cattle with little difficulty. Some were thought to be able to predict the weather.

Regardless of the nature of his workers' talents, a prudent cattle owner would have at least three or four well-seasoned men among his eight cowhands, especially on extensive drives. On an arduous trip of three or four months through rough country, there was no substitute for experienced crew members who knew how to detect stampedes and prevent or stop them, how to fend off or escape Indian attacks, when it was safe to ford swollen rivers, and so on.

It was also very important for the cattle owner to choose men who could work together without conflicts. A harmonious crew was so important on a drive that many cattlemen forbade drinking, gambling, or swearing on the trail. These rules were usually followed—except, perhaps, for the prohibition on swearing. And as with ranch cowboys, the demands of their jobs often forced trail drivers to abandon or transcend any prejudices they might harbor against black comrades, who usually made up about a quarter of a drive crew. "On a drive," says Dale, "a cowboy's ability to do his work, to handle his share and a little extra, was far more important than his color."

There was another reason for such harmony: the scarcity of skilled workers. Many of the best cowhands were black, and "in the beginning, with literally millions of cattle and few experienced cowboys, trail bosses could not afford the luxury of unbridled discrimination," Dale reports.

This "code of the West," as it is often called, was one of the forces that helped ensure a crew's survival and a drive's success. Though often competitive, the average cowboy would not hesitate to come to the aid of another who was in danger. And in a crew of only 11 men, who were responsible at all times of the day and night for 2,500 longhorn, one could not afford to slack off. "In times of crisis," notes Dale, "the cowboy stayed in the saddle indefinitely."

Nor could a cowboy afford to become too sick to work. Many would simply remain at their posts, regardless of illness or grave injury. Among the most stoic workers were black cowboys, and in one instance, a black cowboy's allegiances to his fellow cowhands reached extraordinary—and deadly—lengths:

> We had a negro cowboy named George who was not very well clad because he liked to pike at monte [play cards] too well to buy clothes. We all had colds and coughs till it was like a bunch of Texas pot hounds baying a 'possum when we tried to sleep. One bitter night I was near George on herd [on watch for the night] and tried to get him to go to the chuck wagon and turn his horse loose, but he was too game for that. His teeth were chattering as he said to me, "I can stand it if the rest of you all can." Presently I saw him lean over his saddle horn, coughing, and he looked like he was losing his breath. By the time I got to him he was off his horse, as dead as a mackerel and as stiff as a poker. He had simply frozen to death sitting on that horse. We placed his body in the chuck wagon on his bed and . . . on the highest hill we could find we planted the poor black boy, rolled in his blankets. The ground was sandy; so we could dig a grave deep enough that the coyotes would not claw into it.

4

Trail Drives and Cattle Towns

ONCE THE HERD WAS cut and branded, the crew selected, and the supplies gathered, the cattle owner would set a date—usually in early April—to begin the cattle drive. The first few days of cattle-driving were critical for the foreman, who had to assess the crew's expertise under working conditions and "road break" the cattle, which were unused to trail travel.

Some trail bosses believed in driving the cattle hard for the first few days to wear them out and make them more docile. Others believed in taking it easy at first to allow the herd to become accustomed to walking long distances. Regardless of the method used, however, it was vitally important to avoid or check stampedes, especially in the early days of the drive. One stampede often made the cattle more nervous and thus more likely to stampede again with less provocation. If the herd remained relatively manageable during the first few days, the drive usually settled into a routine of sorts. Still, the

On a trail drive, cattle had to be watched at all times to prevent stampedes or other troubles. Here, cowhands on night watch awaken relief hands for the second guard.

crew had to be vigilant at all times.

The daily schedule on a trail drive was fairly regular. The cook rose first to make coffee and biscuits for the crew. The wrangler awoke early as well to begin rounding up the horses for the other men. Next, the relief hands awoke, ate quickly, and rode out to relieve the night guards, who returned to camp to eat breakfast and change horses before starting another workday. The cattle were left to graze.

A few hours later, around 9:00 a.m., the animals were coaxed into a moving column about a mile long. Two men rode at point, or near the front of the line, to direct the herd; four others rode at swing and flank—back and forth or on both sides of the herd—to keep the cattle properly strung out and to catch stragglers. At drag in the rear of the column, two or three men would prod sluggish, weak, or footsore animals.

The foreman, meanwhile, usually rode ahead by some distance, surveying the route to be sure that it was passable for the wagon and seeing that the crew and herd did not come too close to other herds that might be traveling in advance of his own. At the same time, the wrangler looked after the horses, which traveled beside the cattle.

As the drive began, the cook washed up, cleaned and packed the camp, extinguished the campfire, and hitched his mules to the wagon. He then drove from five to seven miles ahead of the herd and stopped near a water source, as directed by the foreman or scout, to start unpacking and preparing lunch. He followed the same routine after lunch, stopping at a suitable campsite for dinner. Just before sundown, the riders ate in two shifts; those on night duty were served first. By this time, the cattle were watered for the second time and would begin to lie down and rest. Two riders would sing to them to help them settle down.

The first watch of night duty, the most desired

shift, ended at around 11:00 P.M. Middle watch, from 11:00 until 2:00 A.M., was considered the most trying, because the cattle would rise and stretch and riders had to keep them from wandering off. The third and last night shift lasted from 2:00 until dawn. Cowboys estimated time by tracking the positions of the stars, and they would wake the man assigned to the next watch. In this way, each crew member had at least two full nights of sleep every week, barring stampedes or other troubles. When such problems arose, all hands stayed in their saddles all night.

Heavy rain was one of the most trying complications on cattle drives. Sometimes the trail became almost impassable for the wagon, and high, muddy,

Central to every cattle drive was the chuck wagon. In addition to provisions and sleeping rolls, the chuck wagon also carried medicine and "curative" whiskey.

and treacherous river currents carried floating branches and hid sharp rocks and snags. Under such conditions, forcing cattle and horses to struggle across a river became even more arduous and might take an entire day.

Curiously, most cowboys either did not know how to swim or were not strong swimmers, so they were often compelled to find other ways to save themselves in raging waters. R. F. Galbreath, a cowboy from Devine, Texas, remembered crossing the swollen Red River in 1873 with his crewmate Tony Williams, a black cowhand riding point. Williams was in midriver when he was knocked off his horse by a wave. "He disappeared into the river, far beyond reach of the other cowboys, who feared that

Under an ominous sky, cowboys struggle to move cattle across a river. Foul weather not only made a trail more difficult to navigate, it also made the threat of a stampede more likely.

he had drowned," Galbreath recalled. "But in a little while we discovered him holding on to the tail of a big beef steer, and when the steer went up the bank Tony was still holding on and went with him."

Bad weather often brought other disasters as well. Thunder, lightning, or even electrically charged air might trigger a stampede, so all cowboys remained on watch throughout the night to keep restless animals from taking fright and scattering the rest of the herd. Each trail rider was equipped with tarps, extra blankets, slickers, and other supplies for such weather.

Cattle drives entering Indian Territory met other obstacles. Of the several dozen Native American tribes that crews might encounter in the region,

A Dodge City dance hall in 1878, during the town's heyday as a cattle town. The bartender is George Masterson, brother of the local sheriff, "Bat" Masterson.

each could demand several head of cattle as payment for allowing the herd to graze their reservation. Trail bosses risked provoking an attack or a deliberately instigated stampede if they did not comply. But they also had to avoid paying too generously; otherwise, word would spread rapidly along the trail to other tribes ahead of the drive, who would then ask for even higher payments. Overly liberal "donations" would seriously reduce a herd's size and would ultimately cost its owner a great deal of money.

Some cattle drives crossing through Indian Territory would stop for a few days to fatten the herd on the rich grass. The brief period of rest was an enjoyable time for hardworking cowboys, who could finally catch up on their sleep or find a swimming hole in which to wash and cool off. They might also gather food that they would not normally have access to, such as pecans, berries, greens, and honey, or they would have time to fish or hunt turkey and deer. Because of regulations, however, cattle drives that stayed for more than 10 days in Indian Territory were chased off the land by government agents of the Department of the Interior.

Since visits to towns were infrequent during drives, a range rider sought his recreation on the prairie. Nearly every camp stocked a few books or magazines, and some hands knew how to play musical instruments like the violin, guitar, or banjo. Nearly all enjoyed singing; some cowboys were famous among their peers for their excellent voices or their repertoire of songs. Among them were a number of African Americans. A cowboy named John Young gave a firsthand account of Sam, his outfit's black cook: "He always had a cheerful word or a cheerful song, and he seemed to have an affection for every one of us," he related. The tale goes on:

> Sam was also an entertainer. He carried along a banjo, which he played until one of the boys accidentally stepped on it. Then the crew chipped in and bought him a fiddle, which he also played, picking or sawing out airs like "Green Corn, Green Corn."
>
> Carrying 225 pounds at thirty-five, Sam had become too heavy and a bit too old for the active life of a cowboy, but he was still a good rider. . . . He was also part of the general hell-raising of a happy camp. One day, for instance, one of the boys looked at Sam's great bulk and said that Sam was "too big and strong for a man but not big enough for a horse." At that Sam said *he was a horse* and that he would give a dollar to any man in the outfit who could ride him without spurs. . . . One after another the cowboys took off their boots and mounted his back. One after another they were thrown into the soft sand by the human "horse" who could anticipate and bewilder the reactions of his riders. No one earned a dollar that night.

As Kansas grew more populous with farmers unwilling to allow cattle to cross their lands, and as Native American tribes demanded higher tolls

With Willie Kennard and Bass Reeves, Neely Factor (third from left) was among a number of African-American lawmen who helped to maintain order in cowtowns and mining towns during the late 19th century.

for crossing the reservation lands, trails shifted farther west. By 1872, only a few years after Abilene had been established as a major cattle marketplace, a new trail had been blazed: the Western Trail. At the trail's end was Dodge City, Kansas, which had replaced Abilene as a main cattle center. Like Abilene, Dodge City became a stopping place for drives traveling north. And for those crews who reached the end of their journey and delivered their cattle, their pay—and a few nights of raucous fun—awaited them there.

When they arrived at their destination, cattle drivers held the herd on the prairie outside town while the foreman went in to make arrangements with a railroad or cattle broker. These terminus towns were important trading centers for two reasons: they were not only gathering points for railroad shipments of cattle, they also served as exchanges for northern ranchers, who would travel to these towns to purchase cattle and hire men to drive them farther north.

By catering to the needs of visiting ranchers, cowboys, and others who made their living from cattle trading, cowtowns grew explosively within very limited periods of time—often within the span of only two or three years. Saloons, theaters, dance halls, clothing and feed stores, hotels, and gambling houses all sprung up around the ends of well-traveled cattle trails.

Cattle drives heading to the far North followed trails that had been blazed even farther west than the Chisholm or the Western. On these trails they were able to avoid heavy traffic, quarantine rules in the populous areas of Kansas, and some of the tolls charged by Native Americans in Indian Territory. Those bound for the distant North could not afford to be hindered by delays. They had great distances to travel to reach their destinations before the harsh northern winter set in.

As trails moved farther west, the rank of "busiest cattle town" shifted from city to city. Cowboys led rough lives; they worked hard, and many of them played hard as well. As each new crew of cowboys arrived in town, the people and the establishments there would graciously endeavor to lighten their pockets. Noise and bustle and colorful people seemed to follow cowboys and cattle dealers wherever they went. In its heyday, Abilene became famous—and infamous—for its liveliness. One observer described it as "the wickedest and most God-forsaken place on this continent."

But every cattle town also had settlers who did not like the chaos or lawlessness that came with being a commercial center. Famous American gunmen like Bat Masterson, Wild Bill Hickok, and Wyatt Earp and his brothers earned their reputations serving as lawmen in towns like Dodge City; Deadwood, South Dakota; and Tombstone, Arizona, during the years these towns were rough and "uncivilized." Among the ranks of such legendary lawmen were also African-American men, who volunteered or were recruited to keep the peace in cowtowns and mining towns.

In present-day Oklahoma, several all-black towns were established that became notable for being more peaceful than most frontier towns of comparable size. Katz describes one such place, called Boley:

> Although the bustling town . . . rightly claimed it kept the peace far better than other western towns, its history began with violence. A white horse thief shot Dick Shafer, the black town marshal. As Shafer fell from his horse, he fired at the outlaw. Both men died. The Boley Council selected another black man as marshal; since only black families lived in Boley, they had no intention of turning over the vital matter of law and order to someone who did not care about black lives. For the next two years the new marshal did not have to fire his gun or make an arrest. Peace reigned in Boley.

Another account tells of Willie Kennard, a black cavalryman who in 1874 sought the marshal's job in Yankee Hill, Colorado:

> Not only was the town ruled by hardened crooks, the mayor told him, but white citizens might drive him out before the criminals. Kennard insisted on having a chance and the mayor proposed an impossible task—arrest a desperado named Caswit who had raped a teenager and shot her father. At Gaylord's saloon Kennard confronted Caswit. The outlaw drew his Colt .44s only to have Kennard blast them out of his hands and march him to jail. For three years Marshall Kennard tamed Yankee Hill and then rode into the sunset.

Among the most famous African-American lawmen was Bass Reeves, who for 32 years served as deputy U.S. Marshal in present-day Oklahoma. Born into slavery in July 1838 near Paris, Texas, Reeves was from an early age fascinated by weapons,

robberies, and killings—so much so that his mother feared he would become a desperado.

He did not, however. Tall, strong, good-natured, and handy with weapons, Reeves was known and respected by all—including his owner, who chose him to be his body servant, or personal companion. He was so agile with firearms that he was forbidden to participate in the turkey shoots held during local fairs and picnics. Reeves also had the unusual habit of singing softly to himself before engaging in a gunfight, so those who knew him scattered when they heard him begin singing. His keen mind and his ability to quickly size up other people would serve him well in his career as a lawman.

Though normally calm and amiable, Reeves had a quick temper. One day, during a heated argument over a card game, Reeves punched his master. Fearing punishment or death, he headed for Indian Territory. But though he was pursued as a runaway slave, he was never captured. Legend has it that

The town council members of Boley, Oklahoma, gather for an official photograph in the early 1900s. "I always felt free here," declared one Boley resident. "Nobody, no white man, could come in and order me around." Boley was one of dozens of all-black towns that sprang up from Kansas to California after the Civil War.

One of the most famous African-American lawmen of the Old West, Bass Reeves was known and respected throughout Indian Territory. He would often disguise himself as a cowhand, a drifter, or an outlaw to apprehend criminals; during his 32 years as a U.S. Marshal, only one fugitive managed to elude him.

witnesses and those who knew about the incident between Reeves and his master refused to reveal what had happened.

Whether or not the story is true, in 1875 Reeves was offered the post of deputy U.S. Marshal in Fort Smith, Arkansas Territory, becoming one of the first African Americans west of the Mississippi River to receive a commission. He was also one of the first men to serve in the jurisdiction of Judge Parker, famous in the region as the "hanging judge" because of his tendency to dole out death sentences.

Reeves's physical strength was legendary as well. Riding through the Chickasaw Nation one day, he discovered some cowboys trying to pull a steer from a bog along a tributary of the Red River. They were having little success: having roped the steer around its neck, they were attempting to drag it onto land using their horses. But the steer was buried up to its neck in mud, and it was choking from the effort. When Reeves arrived, the cowboys were debating whether or not to give up the animal for dead and put it out of pain by shooting it.

Without a word, Reeves dismounted and began removing his clothes. He then waded into the bog toward the floundering animal and removed the ropes from around its neck. Talking in a low, calm voice to the steer, he grabbed its horns and "pulled and heaved and lifted and grunted" until he was half immersed himself. Stopping only briefly to catch his breath, he kept pulling at the animal until the suction of the bog released the front of the steer and it began to help itself.

Finally, "with great convulsive twists and turns," the steer was extricated. Upon reaching solid ground, "the steer, with not so much as a glance at its savior, wobbled off into the brush and disappeared, bawling its triumph for all the Chickasaw Nation to hear."

Still silent, Reeves climbed out of the bog,

scraped himself off, stuffed his clothes into his saddlebags, and rode off. The only sound he'd uttered, other than the grunts of his efforts to free the steer, were a few mumbled words about "damn dumb cowboys" as he rode away.

Not all African Americans in the West were as honorable as Reeves. Cranford Goldsby, nicknamed "Cherokee Bill" because of his mother's mixed ancestry, became the black equivalent of Billy the Kid—an outlaw who, in his brief life, committed many heinous crimes. Goldsby's father had served in the famed 10th U.S. Cavalry, an elite all-black division assigned to the Far West, and Cranford had been born on a military reservation in Texas. From an early age, his mother impressed upon him the importance of self-defense. "Stand up for your rights," she told him. "Don't let anybody impose on you."

Goldsby's parents separated when he was very young; his mother remarried when he was 12. Feeling alienated and out of place in his new family, the boy began keeping "bad company." Six years later, he shot and wounded a black man after a fist fight.

Soon after that incident, he became a scout for the Cherokee and then for the Creek and Seminole Indians. But in 1894, he joined the notorious outlaw Cook brothers. Because of his race, he was able to travel undisturbed through Indian lands, a route that whites would not have been able to take without fear of attack. Before he turned 20, he was captured and sentenced to die in Arkansas by Judge Parker.

The average black frontiersman was neither a hero nor an outlaw. Like their white counterparts, black cowboys occasionally got into trouble, and at times some became unruly or menacing and deserved arrest. What we consider dangerous and terrifying, however, might have been seen as merely mischievous in the Old West. Most cowhands only intended to have a bit of fun after months of lonely and rigorous work on the trail, as this tale of Abilene in 1870 illustrates:

> A Texas outfit camped on Mud Creek [about a mile from Abilene] had a Negro cook who rode into town and quickly drowned his memories of smoking fires and hungry cowboys with heavy draughts of Abilene whiskey. Then he began shooting up the town—not doing much damage, but making a lot of noise. The town marshal came running and, as one account has it, "managed by some unaccountable good luck" to arrest the cook and throw him into jail. There the cook stayed until his hungry trail crew learned where he was. They mounted, rode into town, drove the marshal into hiding, shot the lock off the door and freed the cook. Then "they galloped past the office of Theodore Henry, chairman of the town trustees, and shot it full of holes." Finally, having rescued one of their own men and expressed their contempt for the town's government, they rode back to camp. Thus a Negro posted two records: he was the first man thrown in the new jail, and the first man to break out.

The cattle town of Cheyenne, Wyoming, also endured such pranks by cowboys. One of them, Bill Walker, described his crew's antics. A very small town, Cheyenne nevertheless had several saloons and its own clothing store with a plate-glass front, "the only mirror that a lot of those cowboys had ever looked into." After a long cattle drive, Walker and his colleagues spent several days in Cheyenne drinking, gambling, and cavorting with women. They returned to their herd but, feeling resentful over having spent their pay, they planned a final foray into the town before taking up the trail again.

Another member of the crew was a cowboy named Bronco Sam, a "genuine black buckaroo" who "wasn't afraid of anything," according to Walker. Bronco Sam was persuaded to ride into Cheyenne on a large, saddled longhorn that had been picked from the herd. The crew accompanied him, "whooping and hollering and swinging knot-

ted ropes to drive the bucking steer," and by the time they arrived, the poor animal was frantic. Spying itself in the window of the clothing store, it panicked and charged "through the window, down the aisles, over the counters, around the shelves—with the clerks diving into corners for protection." With Bronco Sam still holding on, the steer charged back out through the window frame, trailing "pants, coats, underwear, and other odds and ends of gearin'."

Perhaps the crew felt the sting of their own code of honor, however. After they returned the steer to the herd, they rode back into town to make amends before leaving Cheyenne. The amount of damage—

The bustling cattle town of Cheyenne, Wyoming, during the early 1880s, where Bronco Sam stirred up trouble by riding a longhorn into town accompanied by his fellow cowhands.

$350—was cheerfully paid by Bronco Sam, and the townspeople were placated.

Less innocent entertainment was also readily available in cattle towns: nearly every one of them had at least one brothel. Though citizens and lawmen attempted to curb such activity by passing ordinances against brothel owners, the laws only forced the establishments to move beyond town limits, where they were still readily accessible to patrons. (In Abilene, for example, the "Devil's Addition," as the district was known, was situated about a mile northwest of the town.) During winter months, when few visitors passed through, the women employed there went elsewhere for work, returning the following spring with the new season of cattle driving.

Such enterprises drew "riffraff" into cattle towns, but most of the cowboys who passed through were law-abiding. Some did not even drink or gamble. Many went into town to get a good haircut and a bath, to buy new clothes and gear, and to dance or listen to music. The "boothill" cemeteries of the Old West that tourists visit today harbor not cowboys but "gamblers, toughs, and desperadoes who made a point of following new frontiers." Yet because they were often willing to try anything and because they frequently reacted to affronts or slights by townspeople, cowboys earned a reputation for lawlessness.

For cowboys, entering dangerous territory or cowtowns unarmed was not always desirable. Some outlaws and others of questionable integrity would not flinch at shooting an unarmed man. The first man to lose his life in Dodge City was a black cowboy named Tex, "whose only mistake was standing in a crowd on the street during some minor excitement." In the gunfire that followed, Tex was shot, and though his death was believed to be accidental at the time, a gambler named Denver admitted years later that he had shot Tex "just to see him kick."

For this reason, many cattlemen carried guns on the trail. Most favored the .45 caliber Colt revolver—the famous "Colt 45" so often seen in movies about the Old West. But each would commonly carry only one, not two, and it was usually not worn slung across the hips. In fact, cowboys often kept their guns wrapped in their bedrolls. The weapons were heavy and unwieldy and interfered at times with a cowboy's work. And with the exception of cooks, few cowhands were particularly good shots. Only in emergencies or while riding through perilous ranges would they wear revolvers, sometimes supplemented by Winchester rifles strapped across their saddles.

Some cattlemen purposely traveled unarmed, despite the risk. They believed that carrying a gun invited trouble and that it was unnecessary to defend oneself with a weapon. Though regularly featured in movies and stories of the Old West, gunfights were extremely rare. One cowboy, John Arnot, who spent 60 years on the Texas plains, never saw a gunfight—even though he lived for some time in the notoriously violent cattle town of Old Tascosa. Other cowboys loathed the idea of taking another's life—or simply preferred to focus on their work and avoid gunplay.

5

Black Cowboys

A FEW BLACK COWBOYS enjoyed particular fame—or notoriety—during the post-Reconstruction period. Among them was Jim Simpson, who worked for the Flying E Ranch in Wyoming. Simpson earned a reputation as the best roper on the open range. He also established himself as a kind of cowboy sage, admired for his philosophical insights and his encyclopedic command of practical knowledge. If a young cowboy got sick from drinking alkali water, for example, he could find out from Simpson that tomato juice was a good remedy.

One of the most famous cattlemen of the 19th century was a black cowhand named Bose Ikard. Born a slave in Mississippi in 1847, Bose was taken to Texas when he was five by his master's family, where he learned the skills of a cowhand while still a boy.

After the Civil War, Bose was hired by Oliver Loving, an experienced cattleman who was rounding up cattle to drive north. Loving knew the southwestern Plains in great detail, and he knew that traveling directly toward Colorado through the Texas panhandle would invite attacks from the Comanche and Kiowa tribes. While pursuing a dif-

Clad in their work gear, black cowboys from Kansas pose for a studio portrait.

69

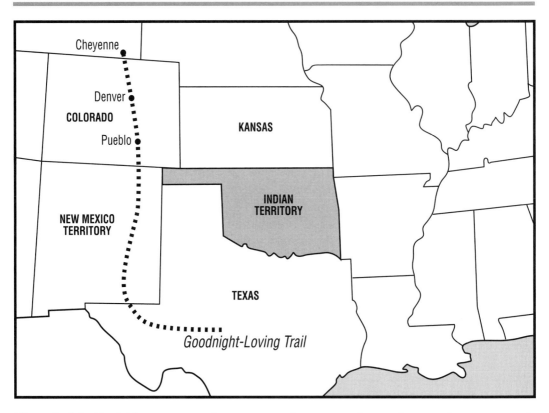

The path of the Goodnight-Loving Trail. The trail's originators aimed to avoid dangerous Comanche and Kiowa territory in the Texas panhandle; by routing cattle drives around the region, they opened up the western cattle market in New Mexico, Colorado, and Wyoming.

ferent route, he met with another cattleman named Charles Goodnight, who was preparing his own drive. Goodnight proposed that they combine their herds—a total of 2,000 head—and drive southwest, toward the Pecos River (which flows through eastern New Mexico and western Texas), before heading north through New Mexico.

The path they took in 1866 became known as the Goodnight-Loving Trail, the westernmost of all the trails founded during the era of the great cattle drives. After selling some of their cattle to the federal government in Fort Sumner, New Mexico, the two men parted ways. Loving continued into northeastern Colorado, where he sold the remaining cattle. Goodnight returned with Bose Ikard to Texas to gather another herd. Goodnight and Bose grew to be great friends, and they were nearly always in one another's company.

Oliver Loving died the following year, and Bose became Goodnight's right-hand man. Goodnight trusted Bose with both his life and his fortune: after cattle were sold, Bose was responsible for carrying and guarding the cash, especially through rough country. "There was a dignity, a cleanliness, and a reliability about him that was wonderful," Goodnight said of Bose:

> His behavior was very good in a fight, and he was probably the most devoted man to me that I ever had. I have trusted him farther than any living man. He was my detective, banker, and everything else in Colorado, New Mexico, and any other wild country I was in. The nearest and only bank was at Denver, and when we carried money I gave it to Bose, for a thief would never think of robbing him—never think of looking in a Negro's bed for money.

Another African-American cowboy named George McJunkin became famous for his contribution to what one noted archaeologist calls "the most important discovery in the field of North American prehistory": the Folsom site, named after the nearby town of Folsom, New Mexico.

Though the facts of his birth and his childhood are unclear, we do know that McJunkin was born into slavery in 1856 in south Texas. He learned how to rope and ride from the vaqueros who worked on his owner's ranch; they also taught him to speak Spanish.

When he was a teenager, he escaped his master by riding away on a mule—believing that a black riding a horse might arouse suspicion. In the virulently anti-black town of Comanche, he bought his first footwear—a pair of cowboy boots—with money he had earned by digging a well. His roping and riding skills landed him a job as a wrangler for a local trail crew, and by the time the drive ended in Dodge City, Kansas, he had earned enough to purchase his own hat, saddle, and horse.

The following spring, he headed back to Comanche to seek another trail job. Along the way, however, he encountered a huge herd of horses being driven west by a man named Gideon Roberds. After McJunkin ran down and lassoed a horse who had escaped the herd, Roberds offered him a job as a breaker.

McJunkin became so adept at training horses to cut out calves from a cattle herd without prompting from their riders, his animals were soon in great demand by ranchers and trail drivers. His skills as a breaker were also sought after. Dr. Thomas E. Owen, one of the partners who owned the famous and enormous 101 Ranch in Oklahoma, hired McJunkin to round up a herd of thoroughbred race horses on a new ranch along the Cimarron River. Owen also hired McJunkin as "wagon boss" for two ranches, with responsibility for 200 horses, thousands of head of cattle, and 100 white cowboys. As a gift for his hard work, McJunkin received a transit —an instrument used by surveyors to mark exact boundary lines.

In the late 19th century, homesteaders who had settled in the West began seeking new types of fencing to protect their fields against grazing cattle herds. Wood was scarce and ineffective; thorny shrubs, such as the osage orange, were often planted as cattle-breaks, but they took time to grow. In 1874, an Illinois farmer named Joseph F. Glidden patented a type of fencing that incorporated bits of jagged metal into strands of wire. Barbed wire, as it came to be known, was enormously popular; in 1885 alone, about 400 patents were issued for barbed wire and machines and other devices that helped install it.

Among those who profited from the new enterprise was George McJunkin, who used his surveying tools to lay off exact boundary lines while supervising the stringing of some of the first fences

Two decades before archaeologists came across these bison bones and this projectile point in Folsom, New Mexico, a black cowboy named George McJunkin discovered similar artifacts in the same region. Though dismissed as unimportant at the time, McJunkin's findings eventually were recognized as one of the most remarkable discoveries in North America.

erected on the open range. His surveyor's skills helped him settle numerous boundary disputes on the high Plains.

McJunkin was working with a large herd of Dr. Owen's cattle in 1889 when he and his crew were waylaid on the open range by a huge blizzard. They managed to find shelter and were snowbound for 10 days. But though the men survived, most of the herd was wiped out and Owen was almost financially ruined. When he died two years later in 1891, McJunkin went to work for a neighboring rancher, William H. Jack.

An avid reader and a quick student, McJunkin had learned to read and write from Roberds's sons, whom he had taught to rope and ride. While McJunkin was working for Jack, Jack's wife gave him a small library of books, including an encyclopedia and numerous works on astronomy and other sciences. McJunkin pored over his new books and even memorized long sections of them. He had a special interest in archaeology and spent hours of his free time digging for fossils and bones, which he added to his growing collection of natural curios.

McJunkin had also acquired a telescope—either from a retired army engineer or from an army paymaster as thanks for saving him from bandits. Whatever its source, the telescope became a treasured possession. McJunkin ordered a leather sheath made for the telescope, and he never rode without it. During the day, when he could not use it to study the stars, he used it to determine the brands on faraway cattle.

In 1908, the town of Folsom, New Mexico, was devastated by a flood. While checking the range for damage, McJunkin discovered a deep slice in an area known as Wild Horse Arroyo, where he had often dug for fossils. This time, however, he came across an unusual find: "great knobby joints and leg bones for animals twice the size of the biggest steer on the ranch," according to Bern Keating in *Famous American Cowboys*.

Wildly excited, McJunkin carried the bones back to the ranch and researched them, telling everyone he could about his wonderful and mysterious discovery. Not until 10 years later, however, in the winter of 1918, did he travel back to the site with a friend. The two collected more bones and a spear point. But though a local amateur archaeologist showed the finds to the Colorado Museum of Natural History in Denver, the experts there were uninterested.

When McJunkin was 65, his house burned, destroying his well-loved collections. Around the same time he took ill, and he died the following year on January 21, 1922. Four years later, Dr. J. D. Figgins of the Denver Museum, who had heard about McJunkin's curious finds, traveled to the Wild Horse Arroyo.

Scientists of this period believed that Native Americans had come from Asia to North America 3,000 years earlier. What the digging crew discovered at the Folsom site, however, revolutionized archaeological assumptions about North American prehistory. Almost immediately, they discovered not only the bones of a species of bison that had become extinct 10,000 years earlier, but manmade spear points—a remarkable discovery that all but proved that humans had lived and hunted in North America thousands of years earlier than scientists had thought.

Though later archaeological discoveries have revealed additional clues to the presence of humans in North America, none has been more remarkable than the Folsom point—the small, flaked piece of chert used for prehistoric spearheads—first discovered by a black cowboy.

While George McJunkin is virtually unknown today despite his historical importance, one of the most celebrated black cowboys, Nat Love, achieved fame in part through his own tall tales. His 1907 autobiography, *The Adventures of Nat Love, Better Known in Cattle Country as Deadwood Dick*, records scores of wildly exaggerated adventures.

Born a slave in Tennessee in 1854, Love left home at 15 and began working the trails. His roping and riding skills earned him a job as a cowpuncher out of Dodge City, where he earned the nickname "Red River Dick." On July 4, 1876, Love won an impressive victory in roping, riding, and shooting contests at a rodeo held in Deadwood, South Dako-

The irrepressible cowboy Nat Love once boasted, "I carry the marks of 14 bullet wounds . . . any one of which would be sufficient to kill an ordinary man."

ta. In tribute to his great skills, he says in his auto-biography, his fellow competitors nicknamed him "Deadwood Dick." (Somewhat confusingly, he was one of several figures in the Old West with this nickname, perhaps because of a popular series of "dime novels" whose central character was called Deadwood Dick.)

In subsequent years, Love had a series of wild adventures. Once, while riding alone looking for stray cattle, he encountered a band of Yellow Dog Indians. After engaging in a shootout with them, he was captured, but he escaped by stealing one of the Indians' horses. On another occasion he used his roping skill to save the life of a fellow cowboy who had fallen with his horse into a raging river. On still another, he and companions from his crew defeated several other outfits in a series of horse races that won them thousands of dollars.

In his autobiography, Love professed to have been adopted by an Indian tribe. He also claimed that he once rode 100 miles on an unsaddled horse in less than 12 hours and that he nearly succeeded in roping and stealing a cannon belonging to the United States Army. On another occasion, he claimed, he rode into a saloon in Mexico and requested two drinks—one for himself and one for his horse.

Of all his achievements, Love was probably proudest of having survived numerous shootings. "I carry the marks of 14 bullet wounds," he once boasted, "any one of which would be sufficient to kill an ordinary man, but I am not even crippled." Boasting that he "gloried in the danger" inherent in the settling of the West, he asserted, "Horses were shot from under me, men killed around me, but always I escaped with a trifling wound at the worst."

In 1889, as the cattle industry began to decline, Love retired from the range to become a Pullman porter. Very few records of the Old West verify his supposed exploits. He claimed that "cattle kings of the West as well as scores of bad men all over the western country" knew him by Red River Dick, yet none of those who spoke about their experiences in settling the West recalled Love at all. Nor do any of the cattlemen or cowboys with whom he claimed to

Ned Huddleston, better known as Isom Dart, was a kind-hearted cattle rustler who loved children and once took a wounded sheriff to the hospital before turning himself in. Dart's luck ran out at age 51, when he was shot in the back by a notoriously cruel cattle detective.

have worked appear in records of the period.

Regardless of the accuracy of his tales, Love's account is the only autobiography of an African-American cowhand. And though he may have vastly overstated his escapades, he nevertheless appears to have been a skilled roper and rider and an extremely colorful character, who worked with—or at least talked with—men who had ridden on cattle drives.

Among the black cowboys who achieved some measure of fame was the fascinating Ned Huddleston, better known as Isom Dart. Though he tried a number of times to go straight, he became known not as a cowhand but as a cattle rustler.

Huddleston was born in Arkansas in 1849 as a slave, like most black cowboys. As a young boy foraging for Confederate officers during the Civil War, Ned gained experience in thievery. After the war ended, he worked briefly as a rodeo clown in southern Texas and Mexico before joining forces with a young Mexican cattle rustler to sell stolen cattle in Texas.

"No man understood horses better," one settler said, recalling Huddleston's bronco-busting years at Charcoal Bottom on the Green River. "I have seen all the great riders," another attested, "but for all around skill as a cowman, Isom Dart was unexcelled." But though Ned gave up rustling for a time, before long he joined the infamous Gault gang, a band of cattle thieves led by Tip Gault and including Jack Leath, Joe Pease, and Terresa, an old friend of Ned's.

The gang spotted a herd of California horses being driven east toward Wyoming and resolved to rustle the herd. But in the process, Joe Pease was struck down by an errant horse. While Ned was burying Pease, he heard shots. His gang had been ambushed by an angry rancher and all of its members were killed. He survived by hiding for the night next to the body of his friend in the grave he had dug.

Weeks later, having been wounded stealing a horse, and collapsing from exhaustion and loss of blood, Ned Huddleston arrived in Green River City, where he resolved to leave the area, change his name, and go straight for good. He boarded a westbound train with all the gang's money and a new name—Isom Dart. Over the next few years, he wandered back to Oklahoma and raised cotton.

Though Dart was a criminal for most of his life, he was known to have an easygoing nature and was especially fond of children. "He used to 'baby-sit' me and my brother when Mother was away or busy," one man recalled. He spent long hours amusing children with songs he had learned as a slave and performances from his days with a Mexican rodeo. And although he was arrested many times, he was never jailed. On one occasion, Dart's integrity won his acquittal:

> [Dart] was arrested by a deputy sheriff [named Joe Philbrick] from Sweetwater County, Wyoming. The deputy's buckboard ran off the road injuring the deputy but leaving Dart unscathed. Prisoner Dart gave the deputy first aid, calmed the horses, lifted the buckboard onto its wheels, drove the deputy into Rock Springs, Wyoming, and left him at the hospital. Then Dart left the buckboard at the stable and turned himself in at the town jail. In a land where cattle rustling was commonplace, such behavior was proof of innocence and he was released.

Eventually, Dart settled into bronco-busting again, and in this way, he managed to trade horses for cattle and build a ranch of his own in Brown's Hole, Wyoming—though he was not above rustling an occasional steer or horse to succeed.

Around this time, Wyoming cattlemen hired a range detective—a brutal and notorious man named Tom Horn—to scout out rustlers. Under the name of Hicks, Horn would ingratiate himself with rustlers before killing them. "A competent cowboy and a companionable man, he found it easy to win the confidence of his intended victims," Keating relates. "Soon he was working and riding with them, and perhaps he joined them in rustling cattle."

When Horn reached the Brown's Hole area, he

sent anonymous notes to suspected rustlers warning them to leave the country or be killed. Although many of them took the threat seriously and left, Dart remained, and he "urged his followers to stand up like men to the assassin, whoever he was." In 1900, Dart was ambushed and killed by Horn, who was hanged three years later for killing a 14-year-old boy.

6

Show Business

Legendary black cowboy Bill Pickett, in his show finery, poses with his horse Croppie, which he named for its cropped left ear.

BY THE BEGINNING of the 20th century, barbed-wire fences had closed off the open range. Overgrazing, a fall in beef prices, the closing of federal lands, and a few terrible droughts sent the cattle industry into decline. The ranches that stayed in business stopped staging long cattle drives to Kansas, Nebraska, the Dakotas, and Montana, relying instead on railroad transportation alone. Demand for cowhands fell, and most cowboys were displaced.

Both black and white cowboys turned increasingly to working on ranches and in traveling shows. "Wild West" shows began touring Mexico, the eastern United States, and Europe, playing to crowds who had never seen real cowboys or witnessed the work they did on the range. Of the black cowboys who joined such shows, Bill Pickett had the most success. Pickett was considered the master of "bulldogging"—subduing a steer by seizing its horns, forcing it to the ground, and then biting its upper lip. In fact, in parts of Texas Pickett is still honored as the inventor of this art. For years he toured with other famous cowboys from the 101 Ranch (including Roy Rogers and Tom Mix), wrestling steers in such varied locales as Madison Square Garden,

Mexico City, and London.

Cowhands had always held contests among themselves for the best roper, fastest brander, best all-around cowpuncher, and other accomplishments, but these competitions, known as rodeos, did not become public shows until the 1890s. Durham and Jones describe the origins of such exhibitions:

> When times were dull or work was slack, it was a common occurrence for one cowboy to try to outdo another in riding or roping. Occasionally the members of an outfit competed for a pot they made up among themselves [out of their wages], but there were always those who tried to rope any steer or ride any bronc just for the hell or the glory of it. . . . [Despite Nat Love's claim] there are relatively few accounts of early formalized contests.

As in the days of trail-driving and range-riding, discrimination and prejudice against black cowboys by their white counterparts was relatively rare. Racial discrimination still plagued black performers in the early years of rodeo competitions, however. Many show outfits forbade black participants entirely.

Bill Pickett, for example, was forced to disguise himself as a Mexican bullfighter until he became famous for bulldogging. He was vindicated decades after his death, however: in 1971, Pickett became the first black voted into Oklahoma City's Cowboy Hall of Fame, and in 1987 a bronze statue of the renowned bulldogger at work was unveiled at the Fort Worth Cowtown Coliseum.

Perhaps the most spectacular rodeo activity, bulldogging was popularized (and presumably invented) by black cowboys. During the era of trail driving, cowboys frequently had to rope and bring back into the fold steers that broke from the rest of the herd. At times a cowboy either forgot or did not carry his rope and was forced to bring the steer down

Bill Pickett demonstrates his unique version of the art of bulldogging, now a standard event in modern rodeos.

by hand. This practice, known as "throwing" a steer, involved seizing the animal's horns and twisting the neck to throw it off its feet.

It is unclear where the term "bulldogging" originated. One theory holds that at first cowboys grabbed not the horns but the nose of a steer—as bulldogs, which were first developed in England to fight bulls, might do to their quarry. And though modern dictionaries record that the term was coined in 1907, several cowhands recall bulldogging being practiced as early as the 1870s. A cattleman named Ed Nichols reported the bulldogging efforts of one black cowhand, an employee of the prominent cattleman Bill Hudson, who had traveled to Texas to purchase longhorns for a trail drive:

> At the end of one day of buying, Hudson's cattle were all rounded into one herd, and the men sat down to eat. Suddenly a steer broke out of the herd and could not be driven back. A man from each outfit mounted his horse and attempted to rope the steer, but without success. A Negro cowboy named Andy, "one of Hudson's main trail riders and ropers," could not find his lariat, so in desperation he took after the steer without a rope. "Riding up to it, he reached down with both hands and caught its nose in one hand and a horn in the other. He twisted the steer's nose up and threw him, jumping from the saddle as he did so. It was the first bulldogging I ever saw."

Another cattleman, Harry Chrisman, described a similar technique used by a black cowboy named Sam Johnson, who "bulldogged a Texas longhorn with horns spreading six feet. Those who saw Johnson's performance thought they had seen one of the best cowboy shows in central western Kansas."

The most famous bulldogger in American history, however, is Bill Pickett. Zack Miller, his boss, called Pickett "the greatest sweat-and-dirt cowhand that ever lived—bar none. . . . [W]hen they turned Bill Pickett out," Miller claims, "they broke the mold."

Pickett himself, "a big-handed, wild-riding South Texas brush-popper," claimed to have invented the sport of bulldogging, though evidence seems to prove otherwise. But his style was "so startling and so effective" that he is often still credited as the originator. At any rate, he is generally acknowledged as the foremost practitioner of the sport.

According to several sources, Pickett began by riding his favorite horse, Spradley, alongside the steer and then jumping from his mount, flying through the air to grab hold of the steer's horns. Then he would twist the animal's nose skyward, attach his teeth to its lip, and fall to one side, using his jaw and neck muscles to force it to the ground. He would finish his remarkable demonstration by raising his hands in the air to show that he was holding the half-ton steer solely by the strength of his teeth.

Bulldogging was one of five standard events in a rodeo show. (Today's rodeos also include two other categories for female participants.) Contestants compete in bareback bronc-riding, saddle bronc-riding, bull-riding, calf-roping, and steer-wrestling or bulldogging. In bareback riding, a rider tries to hold onto a special rigging to keep himself on the back of an untamed horse, or bronco, while the animal tries to "buck" the rider off its back. Using only one hand, the rider must stay on the horse for a specified amount of time (usually 8 to 10 seconds). If the rider falls or if the free hand touches any part of the rider's or horse's body, the competitor is disqualified. In saddle bronc-riding, a lightweight saddle is used and the rider must hold on to a piece of rope.

The most dangerous event in the rodeo is bull-riding. The Brahma bull is a ferocious and huge animal that can weigh up to 2,500 pounds and is known for its quickness and strength. The rider must keep a one-handed grip for at least 10 seconds on a single bull-rope that circles the animal's trunk. The strength and spirit of the animals is taken into account by judges.

In calf-roping and bulldogging, a contestant attempts to complete a set of maneuvers in the shortest possible time. A calf or steer is released into the arena through a chute and the cowhand pursues on horseback. In calf-roping the contestant must rope the calf's neck, dismount, throw the calf to the ground, and tie its feet while the horse keeps the rope taut. Bulldogging requires that the rider jump from his horse to the steer's back and flip the steer

One of the most famous bronc-busters was black cowboy Jesse Stahl, shown here in a 1930 photo. Though many riders considered Stahl the finest bronc-buster, he often placed lower than white competitors because of his race.

onto its back as quickly as possible.

Rodeo contestants have never received regular fees; as with the informal early competitions held among cowboys who bet their wages on their own skills, rodeo participants compete for prize money alone.

Pickett worked for the famous 101 Ranch,

owned by brothers Zack and "Colonel Joe" Miller. The 101 had acquired several cowhands, including the bronc-buster Johnny Brewer, roper Jim Hopkins, and Pickett, all of whom became so expert that they were eventually considered professionals and forbidden to enter local or regional amateur cowboy contests. So the Miller brothers decided to stage their own shows.

At first they were local performances, held during conventions and gatherings at the 101. But Colonel Joe was eager not only to preserve the customs and traditions of frontier life, but also to show the rest of the country what the "real" Old West was like. A few years later, the 101 went on the road, performing its first big rodeo show in 1905. By 1907 the troupe was calling itself "the most famous representative of the cattle raising business."

Pickett and Spradley were a big hit with audiences in America and abroad. His assistants included two white cowboys, Will Rogers and Tom Mix, who would later make their own names in the business. Pickett, says Katz, "mastered the ferocious in nature not with weapons that inflict pain and death, but through a craftsmanship rooted in respect for life. His innovation—his best monument—has and will continue to provide entertainment for millions."

Among the many adventures of the traveling 101 Ranch crew was their first night performing at New York's Madison Square Garden in 1907. A frightened steer broke loose, and Pickett and Rogers galloped into the spectators' stands to corral the animal. The following year during a Mexico show, Pickett took Zack Miller up on a bet that Pickett couldn't stay on a bull for five minutes. Pickett did—but was nearly killed. "In time," Katz notes, Pickett "broke almost every bone in his body."

The 101 Ranch soon became known around the world, playing in places like Chicago, New York,

London, and Mexico City. As the show grew in popularity, Miller continued to search for expert cowboys to enhance the 101's reputation. Although Will Rogers was not a regular hand on the ranch, he worked with the cowboys of the 101 on road tours. His assistant, a black cowboy named Henry Clay, is credited with having helped the famous roper perfect his craft. Durham and Jones describe how the two worked together:

> As Clay, on a fast horse, rode past Rogers, the horseman called out the horse's foot [that] the roper was to pick up. Eventually Rogers "could make his spinning trick ropes do just about anything but talk."

Show business was different from the cattle business. After a number of years, the traveling 101 Ranch show became a glorious pageant of stereotyped images of the American cowboy. Colonel Joe himself was a star attraction, carrying a "six-shooter" and riding his favorite horse equipped with elaborate gear worth several thousand dollars. The 101 Wild West Show broke new ground in commercial entertainment in America—and was one of the principal inspirations for the Hollywood image of the American cowboy that developed during the 20th century. Lewis Atherton, in *The Cattle Kings*, describes its importance:

> [T]he 101 Wild West Show convinced audiences that ranchers engaged in a continuous round of danger, excitement, and thrilling escapes. It depicted savage Indians massacring helpless whites, being driven off by rescue parties, and staging weird, primitive dances. Trick riding and shooting, bucking broncos, Texas longhorn cattle, buffaloes, the Pony Express, Mexican bandits robbing the Deadwood stage, and vigilantes all passed in review. . . . Even more astounding were the feats of the "cowgirls." . . . Ranch girls often liked to ride, and on small ranches they helped at busy seasons in handling livestock, but as a species "cowgirls" simply did not exist. They lived only in the

West of commercial entertainment. Nevertheless, the English found them fascinating, dressed, as they were, in divided skirts, top boots, and wide, gray felt Stetson hats.

In keeping with the image of American cowhands as range riders, London newspapers reported that the cowboys and cowgirls of the 101 chose to camp out on the showgrounds between performances rather than take lodging indoors.

In later years, the Miller brothers' show featured Russian cossacks, elephants, camels, boomerang-throwing displays, and even "Arabian" dancers and ballerinas. By the time the 101 Wild West Show succumbed to bankruptcy in 1931, Atherton notes, it had "reduced the code of the West to an absurdity never before achieved." Some of the famous cowboys who worked with the 101, including Tom Mix and Will Rogers, had already become film stars, making names for themselves in the "Old West" of Hollywood movies.

The year after the 101 ceased touring, Zack Miller fell ill. Bill Pickett, then in his seventies, was the ranch's only remaining original hand, and he assumed nursing duties for his former boss. He also tried to help with ranching chores. Pickett was roping horses one day, according to one account, when a particularly spirited sorrel reared and dived at him. Pickett dodged, but not quickly enough, and the horse knocked him down, kicked him, and fractured his skull. He died from his injuries less than two weeks later.

Wild West pageants like the 101 were not the only sources behind the mythical image of the all-American cowhand. Many of the legendary exploits that appeared in Hollywood movies grew out of the earliest memoirs of actual cattlemen and their employees. In 1916, for example, George W. Saunders and his associates founded an organization called the Old Time Trail Drivers Association, open

Hailed as one of the first true western stories and a model for hundreds of novels that followed, Owen Wister's book The Virginians *nevertheless includes no black characters.*

Aside from the 101 Ranch Show, the most famous traveling rodeo troupe was Buffalo Bill's Wild West Show, seen here during a dazzlingly chaotic performance in Wyoming. Buffalo Bill's show included stars like Buck Taylor, "King of the Cowboys"; Annie Oakley, "Little Sure Shot"; and for one season, the Sioux chief Sitting Bull.

to Texans and anyone else with connections to the era of trail drives. The group published biographies and firsthand accounts by survivors of trail drives, including tales of "storms, floods, stampedes, Indian troubles, and desperate undertakings." As Atherton relates, many of these stories may have been inaccurate or at least slightly exaggerated, and most were tinged with nostalgia, but they all reflected common experiences:

Trail drivers were whole-souled and big-hearted. Every cowboy was the champion of womanhood. Hospitality abounded. Courage, self-reliance, willingness to take responsibility, and longheadedness marked the successful man. Although often "diamonds in the rough," trail drivers were charitable and chivalrous. A killing in a fair fight went unpunished. Hard work was the lot of most, but those who faced it had a real chance to make good. Far more interested in recording colorful episodes than in considering common characteristics, given to action rather than to ideas, such men analyzed their contemporaries less thoroughly than had [Joseph] McCoy long before, but, like him, they obviously felt that a common role prevailed in the early days.

The cowboy came to represent ruggedness and a simple, commonsense approach to life that typified the best of America. This national icon made no room for an African-American tradition. Regardless of the number of skilled black cowboys that had worked on ranches or ridden the range, the Old West of the movies and of published memoirs, with very few exceptions, simply excluded them. This was due in part to a virulent wave of racism sweeping across the country during the first decades of the 20th century—the period immediately following the decline of the open range and trail driving. One of the most popular books of the time was Thomas Dixon's intensely racist novel, *The Clansman* (1905), on which the motion picture *The Birth of a Nation* was based.

Often considered the first true western story, *The Virginian* was published in 1902 by Owen Wister. The author had visited the West as early as 1885 and had encountered black cowboys in his travels, yet he included no black characters in his book. Wister, note Durham and Jones, probably "shared the racial prejudices of his time and social class," and the book simply ignores the fact that black cowboys existed. But *The Virginian* became "the great archetype that established the Western as a distinct genre of popular fiction. . . . [I]t set the pattern for thousands of short stories, novels, motion pictures and television programs."

One of the readers inspired by Wister's vision of the Old West was a New York dentist named Zane Grey, a masterful storyteller who decided in 1904 to forgo dentistry for writing. In 1908 he published *The Last of the Plainsmen*, and he later won enormous popular success with *Riders of the Purple Sage* (1912). Before his death in 1939, he wrote scores of novels and tales of the West, many of which are still popular today.

But Grey's Old West was as dominated by white cowboys as that of Wister. The characters, settings, and plots of the western novels, movies, and television shows that followed quickly settled into formulas from which black frontiersmen and women were excluded. "The Negro cowboy, in fiction," say Durham and Jones, "was confronted with a color line over which he could not ride."

In the 1940s and 1950s, the black cowhand finally attained at least some measure of literary recognition. Walter Van Tilburg Clark's 1940 novel, *The Ox-Bow Incident*, is set in Nevada cattle country during the 1880s and examines mob violence, centering on the lynching of three innocent black men accused of cattle rustling. The novel was made into a film in 1943. Novels and stories written during this period by lesser-known authors also included black characters: Genevieve Greer's *The Aristocrat*; Tom Lea's *The Wonderful Country*; and Allan R. Bosworth's story "Stampede!", about a cattle drive along the Western Trail into Kansas, which features Dan Robie, a black cowboy.

Despite such notice, the prevailing belief among movie fans and readers for many decades was that the black frontiersman had never existed. Most fiction writers and screenwriters were historically ignorant of—or did not care about—the importance of black cowboys in pioneer America. Many simply assumed that because they had never appeared in western fiction, they did not exist. Durham and Jones comment on one author's claim that "the prairie was different from the city . . . for there the Jew, Negro and Italian never came. . . . [many]

Americans accept [this] as history, and what they learn is strangely incomplete."

Even those in the entertainment and publishing businesses who did study the Old West, however, became locked into the public perception of an all-white American frontier, and they based their decisions on the incorrect concept of a homogenous America. Presenting black or ethnically diverse characters in westerns would appear unrealistic to viewers and readers, they reasoned, because most had never been exposed to the real facts of the American West.

Moreover, because the cowboy had attained the status of folk hero in America, many feared to make

Though not as popular as they were in the early decades of the 20th century, western films now offer more balanced portrayals of the people who settled the West. Here, Clint Eastwood (left) and Morgan Freeman (right) are bounty hunters in the 1992 Warner Bros. film Unforgiven.

Danny Glover (left) and Rick Schroeder (right) in the television miniseries Lonesome Dove, *based on Larry McMurtry's western novel of the same name.*

him "too clearly differentiated from most other Americans." To portray a cowboy as a black man— or an Englishman or a German—would be to risk alienating a large portion of the paying public. Thankfully, such rationalizing is rare today. Although western movies and novels are not as wildly popular as they once were, they tend to be more balanced in portraying the kind of people who worked and settled in the Old West. Popular 1990s westerns like *Unforgiven* and *Lonesome Dove* present a black homesteader and bounty hunter (played by Morgan Freeman) and a black cowboy (played by Danny Glover).

Perhaps more than any other period in U.S. history, the pioneering of the West continues to capture the American imagination. A time of vast open prairies, undiscovered territories, and thrilling adventures, it has become a symbol of an independent and entrepreneurial spirit that many believe is America's alone.

In the process of glorifying the Old West, the extraordinary contributions of African Americans must not be overlooked. The accomplishments of such trailblazers as Esteban, the 16th-century explorer widely believed to be the first black to see the American West; of York, Lewis and Clark's expert interpreter; of the intrepid James Beckwourth; even of the Exodusters, brave men and women who traveled westward to find a better life, provide proof of a long and unrecognized African-American legacy. The skills and ingenuity of thousands of black cowboys, many of whom were former slaves, helped to transform and define the American West.

"Americans have lost something valuable if they forget that Wild Bill Hickok and George Washington Carver grew up on the Western plains at the same time," Durham and Jones point out. "Americans need to remember that the West once nearly approached the democracy that they are still striving to achieve. . . . then maybe American history and fiction can one day be desegregated."

FURTHER READING

Atherton, Lewis. *The Cattle Kings*. Bloomington: Indiana University Press, 1961.

Brown, Dee. *The American West*. New York: Charles Scribner's Sons, 1994.

Burton, Arthur T. *Black, Red and Deadly: Black and Indian Gunfighters of the Indian Territory, 1870-1907*. Austin: Eakin Press, 1991.

Carroll, Joseph. October 1938. William Trail: An Indiana Pioneer. *Journal of Negro History* 23:420-25.

Dale, Edward Everett. *Cow Country*. Norman, OK: University of Oklahoma Press, 1942.

Davis, Henry. October 1938. John Malvin: A Western Reserve Pioneer. *Journal of Negro History* 23:426-34.

de Graaf, Lawrence B. May 1980. Race, Sex and Region: Black Women in the American West. *Pacific Historical Review* 285-313.

Dobie, J. Frank. *Cow People*. Boston: Little, Brown and Co., 1964.

Durham, Philip and Everett L. Jones. *The Negro Cowboys*. Lincoln: University of Nebraska Press, 1965.

Durham, Philip. 1955. The Negro Cowboy. *American Quarterly* 7:291-301.

Katz, William Loren. *The Black West: A Documentary and Pictorial History of the African American Role in the Westward Expansion of the United States*. New York: Simon & Schuster, 1996.

Keating, Bern. *Famous American Cowboys*. Chicago: Rand McNally and Co., 1977.

Love, Nat. *The Life and Adventures of Nat Love, Better Known in the Cattle Country as "Deadwood Dick."* 1907. Reprint, Baltimore: Black Classic Press, 1988.

Meier, August and Elliott Rudwick, eds. *The Making of Black America: Essays in Negro Life and History.* New York: Atheneum, 1969.

Porter, Kenneth W. *The Negro on the American Frontier.* New York: Arno Press, 1971.

_____. Summer 1969. Negro Labor in the Western Cattle Industry, 1866-1900. *Labor History* 346-74.

_____. July 1956. Negroes and Indians on the Texas Frontier, 1831-1876. *Journal of Negro History* 41:185-214.

Rice, Lawrence D. *The Negro In Texas: 1874-1900.* Baton Rouge: Louisiana State University Press, 1971.

Savage, William Sherman. 1940. The Negro in the Westward Movement. *Journal of Negro History* 25:531-9.

_____. 1945. The Negro on the Mining Frontier. *Journal of Negro History* 30:30-46.

_____. 1951. The Role of Negro Soldiers in Protecting the Indian Territory from Intruders. *Journal of Negro History* 36:25-34.

INDEX

INDEX

PICTURE CREDITS

GINA DE ANGELIS earned a B.A. in theater and history from Marlboro College, Vermont, and an M.A. in history from the University of Mississippi in 1997. She is a veteran of the Pennsylvania Renaissance Faire, a re-creation of an Elizabethan English village, and is the author of several plays and screenplays. This is her first book for Chelsea House.